# Ninja® Foodi®
# XL PRESSURE COOKER STEAM FRYER
# WITH SMARTLID™
## COOKBOOK FOR BEGINNERS

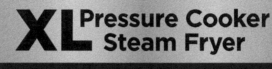

with **SmartLid**

# COOKBOOK FOR BEGINNERS

## 75 RECIPES FOR
### STEAM CRISPING, PRESSURE COOKING, AND AIR FRYING

PHOTOGRAPHY BY HÉLÈNE DUJARDIN

ROCKRIDGE
PRESS

For general information on our other products and services or to obtain technical support, please contact our Customer Care Department within the United States at (866) 744-2665, or outside the United States at (510) 253-0500.

Rockridge Press publishes its books in a variety of electronic and print formats. Some content that appears in print may not be available in electronic books, and vice versa.

Interior and Cover Designer: Patricia Fabricant
Art Producer: Janice Ackerman
Editor: Cecily McAndrews
Production Editor: Andrew Yackira
Production Manager: Martin Worthington

Photography © 2021 Hélène Dujardin. Food styled by Anna Hampton.

Paperback ISBN: 978-1-64876-403-5
eBook ISBN: 978-1-64876-404-2
R1

# CONTENTS

# INTRODUCTION

**SET IT AND FORGET IT IS THE NAME OF THE GAME WITH OUR** new Ninja® Foodi® XL Pressure Cooker Steam Fryer with SmartLid™! Gone are the days of switching between two lids to access different functions: With our new SmartLid™ technology, you can easily toggle between steam and crisp plus 12 other functions by simply moving the SmartLid Slider™. This is the newest, best technology in pressure cooker steam fryers. Just see for yourself!

We're bringing you an entirely new way of cooking in a multi-cooker with our SteamCrisp™ technology. By steaming and crisping at the same time, you can take your air frying to a new level. Not only can you Steam & Crisp your favorite air fryer goodies—like chicken wings and potatoes—but you can also Steam & Crisp larger cuts of meat, like whole chickens or pork. Unlike air frying, this function will tenderize the inside of your proteins while crisping the outside, all under one lid!

As the people who have spent hours tinkering with the Ninja® Foodi® XL Pressure Cooker Steam Fryer with SmartLid™ to bring you these recipes, our favorite part is the ability to build and cook a complete meal at once. Our new SteamCrisp™ technology allows you to stack your main and side dishes to make 2- or 3-part layered meals, so your rice, broccoli, and chicken will be done at the same time and cooked to perfection—no more waiting for a pot of rice to finish cooking, and no extra dishes.

The icing on the cake with the Ninja® Foodi® XL Pressure Cooker Steam Fryer with SmartLid™ is . . . cake (and bread!). That's right: you can also make cake and bread, right in the new Ninja® Foodi®! With our Steam & Bake function, you can make fluffy cakes and baked goods. The steam gives you a moist and delicious result every time, so start with your favorite homemade batters or boxed cakes, and let the steam do the rest. So far as bread goes, Steam & Crisp is perfect for baking homemade or store-bought dough. The steam allows for a higher rise, chewy interior, and crusty exterior, while the crisping function gives you a beautiful golden-brown exterior. The new Ninja® Foodi® will make a bread maker out of you in no time!

With the Ninja® Foodi® XL Pressure Cooker Steam Fryer with SmartLid™, you'll want to get rid of your other kitchen appliances for this amazing all-in-one device. All these recipes are approved by the Ninja® Test Kitchen (and made with love), so keep reading for some great food!

# 1

# Ninja® Foodi® SmartLid™ 101

**THE NINJA® FOODI® XL PRESSURE COOKER STEAM FRYER**
with SmartLid™ is a revolutionary new appliance that will change
the way you cook. It's a multicooker with a huge difference: The
lid does it all. With the SmartLid™, you can Steam & Crisp, Steam
& Bake, Air Fry, and Pressure Cook to make hundreds of recipes.
Even better, you can cook an entire meal in one appliance—protein,
vegetables, and starch. Although there are several other multicookers on the market, the Ninja® Foodi® SmartLid™ is different
because you don't need to change lids depending on the functions
you need. In this chapter, you'll learn about those functions and the
benefits of cooking with the SmartLid™ so you can unleash all this
cooker's potential.

# WHY THE SMARTLID™?

Sounds basic, but it's true: To maximize the potential of different ingredients, various cooking methods are needed. Pressure cooking cooks food quickly and makes foods such as meats very tender in a short period of time, but you won't get that wonderful crispy skin on a pressure-cooked chicken breast. Steaming cooks food gently, maintaining flavor and nutrients, but you can't achieve a crisp edge on Brussels sprouts with just steam. The SmartLid's™ TenderCrisp and Steam & Crisp technology cooks these foods to tender perfection by pressure cooking or steaming and then adding a crisp finish for delicious results every time.

Until now, home cooks have settled for convenience over flavor. Yes, it's easy to just throw food into a pressure cooker or steamer, but the versatility of this appliance lets you have both convenience *and* flavor. The lid lets you switch seamlessly between pressure cooking, steaming, and air frying. Imagine a salmon fillet that is tender and moist on the inside because it has been gently cooked with steam but with a lovely browned exterior because you finished cooking it with the air frying function.

The SmartLid™ is a 14-in-1 appliance that lets you change cooking techniques effortlessly by just moving a slider on the unique lid. You can steam and crisp, steam and bake, proof dough, air fry, bake, roast, broil, dehydrate, sear/sauté, steam, pressure cook, sous vide, make yogurt, and keep food warm. All that adds up to faster, better meals for you, versus Ninja® Foodi® SmartLid™ in dry mode only.

## Steam & Crisp

This function, which is unique to the Ninja® Foodi® SmartLid™, produces different controlled levels of steam to cook the interior of the food while superheated air crisps the outside. This is a brand-new cooking technology that will produce superior results with little effort on your part versus the Ninja® Foodi® SmartLid™ in dry mode only. It can all be done with the Deluxe Reversible Rack and the cooking pot.

Using this Steam & Crisp function, you can make complete meals in 25 minutes or less. The rack lets you layer foods so they cook at the same time and finish quickly. For instance, wouldn't you love to make Pasta with Homemade Sauce and Meatballs (page 172) all in one pot? How about Chicken Marsala with Roasted Red Potatoes (page 135)? With the SmartLid™, you can!

This function also lets you cook large pieces of meat, for example a beef roast or a whole chicken, tenderizing the meat and making the skin crisp. You add half a cup of water to the appliance before cooking, and you'll serve moist but crisp roasts and other foods.

Here's another nifty trick the Steam & Crisp function allows you to do: The SmartLid™ lets you cook bread just like commercial bakeries, with just the right amount of moisture, which is the secret to best results. Make the best Sourdough Bread (page 204), Garlic Dinner Rolls (page 201), and Cheesy Bread Sticks (page 208) you've ever had with this unique function.

## TenderCrisp™

This method uses pressure cooking to cook food quickly and evenly, preserving the nutrients and flavor. After the food is pressure cooked with moist heat, you can use the Air Fry function to crisp the outside of foods for beautifully browned casseroles or chicken potpies, all under one lid.

## Steam & Bake

This unique function lets you combine the gentle heat of steaming with the higher heat of baking, so foods are fluffy and moist on the inside and perfectly done on the outside. Use this function to make foods that don't need a super crisp crust, such as frittatas, fluffy cakes, corn bread, and so much more.

# NINJA® FOODI® SMARTLID™ COMPONENTS

Because the Ninja® Foodi® SmartLid™ is unique and brand-new, it's important to take a little time to familiarize yourself with its components so you can get the most out of your new appliance.

## SmartLid™

This is the component that makes this appliance unique. Once the lid is securely fastened, you use the slider to choose the cooking function. This sturdy and unique three-in-one lid means you don't have to store different lids for different functions, as you do with every other multicooker. Once the function is selected, you can customize cooking by choosing the temperature and time.

## SmartLid Slider™

The SmartLid™ has a slider on the front that lets you choose the perfect function to cook your food. Simply move the slider to effortlessly toggle between the functions. There are three main modes within the slider: Pressure, SteamCrisp, and Air Fry/Stovetop. The slider moves easily and snaps into place. The cooking functions intelligently change as you move from mode to mode.

## Removable Cooking Pot

The removable cooking pot fits perfectly into the unit. Use this pot for all of your cooking in the unit, including to make pasta, Jambalaya (page 125), Miso-Garlic Risotto with Roasted Root Vegetables (page 90), chili, soups, and stews. The pot is ceramic-coated and nonstick for easy cleanup. It is also PTFE- and PFOA-free and is dishwasher safe, but you can also clean it in the kitchen sink.

## Multi-Purpose Pan

The Multi-Purpose Pan is sold separately, but you'll see it used in some recipes. Its unique shape and size (8¾ inches wide by 2¾ inches high) mean that it fits snugly in the appliance for creating

Deluxe Reversible Rack

SmartLid™ Slider

Cook & Crisp™ Basket

SmartLid™

Cooking Pot

14 Cooking Programs

bubbly casseroles and fluffy, moist cakes. The pan is ceramic-coated, nonstick, and PTFE- and PFOA-free for easy cleanup. It is not dishwasher safe, so hand wash only.

## Cook & Crisp™ Basket

When you use the Air Fry function, the air that circulates in the appliance needs to be able to come into contact with all of the food's surfaces. The Cook & Crisp™ Basket holds food securely and lets the appliance crisp up all the edges. This basket has a ceramic coating and is nonstick for easy cleaning. It is also PTFE- and PFOA-free.

## Deluxe Reversible Rack

The Deluxe Reversible Rack is the secret to making entire meals in this appliance. For instance, to cook Banh Mi Bowls with Crispy Tofu (page 94), the grain goes on the bottom of the rack, the veggies in the middle, and the tofu on top. All cook perfectly with just the touch of a button. Or put quinoa on the bottom, broccoli in the middle, and Almond-Crusted Salmon (page 104) on the top for a gourmet meal that is ready in minutes.

## Pressure Release Valve

When you pressure cook, you must release some steam before you can open the appliance. The pressure release valve lets you release pressure quickly, naturally over time, or (on some models of the SmartLid™), on a delay, depending on what you're cooking.

# Steam & Crisp and TenderCrisp™

Steam & Crisp is a function of the new SmartLid™, whereas TenderCrisp™ is a cooking technique that the Foodi® has perfected. By combining steaming or pressure cooking with the unique crisping function, these two ways of cooking will make some of the best food that you've ever tasted—with very little cleanup. You can cook food faster and the results will be juicier and better tasting, versus the Ninja® Foodi® SmartLid™ in dry mode only.

Steam & Crisp uses the steaming and crisp functions together for perfect results. The Steam & Crisp function is best for full multitextured meals, crisping up leftovers, lean proteins, and more delicate foods such as fish. Steam cooks food gently to lock in the nutrients and preserve moisture and flavor. You can make Lemon and Honey Steam-Crisped Whole Chicken (page 130), Eggplant Parmesan with Broccoli and Penne Marinara (page 78), Barbecue Cauliflower Tacos with Cabbage Slaw and Avocado (page 80), Homemade Fish Sticks and Broccoli (page 111), and Spicy Shrimp with Vegetables and Cilantro Rice (page 122) with ease using this function. The possibilities are endless.

The TenderCrisp™ method uses the Pressure Cook function to lock in juices and cook food 40 percent faster than traditional cooking methods. Under pressure, water boils at 250°F rather than the standard 212°F. Food cooks more quickly because the steam is created at a higher temperature. After the food reaches a safe final internal temperature, the Air Fry function is used for a crispy finish. This method is best for large pieces of meat such as roasts, soups and stews, casseroles, and frozen foods. Use the Pressure Cook and Air Fry functions to make Jambalaya (page 125), Miso-Garlic Risotto with Roasted Root Vegetables (page 90), and Korean-Style Sticky Ribs (page 167).

# GET FAMILIAR WITH YOUR FUNCTIONS

The Ninja® Foodi® SmartLid™ has so many functions it may seem overwhelming at first. But once you learn a little bit about this remarkable appliance, using it will become second nature, especially when you cook using the recipes in this book.

The key to the whole appliance is the SmartLidSlider™ on the SmartLid™, which lets you seamlessly transition between pressure cooking, steaming, and air frying. Those functions make this appliance much more powerful and versatile than other countertop appliances. Let's go through each function in more detail.

## SmartLid Slider™

The slider on the Ninja® Foodi® SmartLid™ is prominently featured on the sturdy lid. You just slide it to the function you want to use, whether it's pressure cooking, steam crisping, steam baking, or air frying/stovetop. This slider is the first part you interact with when you use this appliance.

## Pressure Cook

Pressure cooking has been around for centuries. This simple and effective method for cooking food uses the pressure that builds up in a sealed container when steam is generated. The increased temperature inside the appliance cooks food quickly and evenly. The juicy, tender, and delicious results are made even better because super-heated air then crisps the exterior of the food.

## Steam & Crisp

Steaming is generally regarded as one of the healthiest ways to cook food—it involves no added fat, and the food cooks evenly at 212ºF, a lower temperature that gently cooks proteins and starches while preserving the nutrients and flavor.

With this function you can steam and then crisp foods in one pot. Air fryers cook foods by circulating superhot air around the food, which mimics oil frying but with much less fat and calories. The Steam & Crisp function also allows you to make bakery-style breads at home, because the bread cooks and stays moist in the steam heat, while the crisping function develops a satisfyingly crisp crust.

### Steam & Bake

When you want to make the best cookies and cakes, turn to the Steam & Bake function. You will turn out moist cakes and tender cookies in less time than they would take to cook in a traditional oven.

## Air Fry / Stovetop

What's remarkable about this appliance is that you can air fry foods as well as cook them using other traditional functions of a stove and oven.

### Air Fry

Air frying is a fabulous way to cook foods including French fries, baked potatoes, chicken fingers, and snacks. Hot air circulates around the food to crisp it without you having to add any oil or fat.

### Broil

Broiling food exposes it directly to heat. This quick and efficient cooking method brings out the flavor of foods such as steaks and chops and creates a delicious browned crust.

### Bake/Roast

Baking and roasting are dry heat methods of cooking; the only real difference is in the temperature. Roasting cooks foods at a higher temperature, usually 400°F to 450°F, whereas baking takes place at temperatures under 400°F. Cook quick breads, muffins, cookies, and large pieces of meat such as steaks and roasts using this function.

### Dehydrate

Dehydrating food preserves it for long storage times. Make delicious fruit leathers, dried fruits, and jerky for camping and snacks.

### Proof

You can not only bake bread in the Ninja® Foodi® SmartLid™, you can also let it rise—known as proofing—too. Bread dough rises better in a draft-free, warm environment.

### Sear/Sauté

No more pulling out a saucepan or skillet and turning on the stove to sear or sauté foods. Just use this function on your SmartLid™.

### Steam

You can steam foods without using the crisper function, if you'd like. This function is great for steaming delicate veggies.

### Sous Vide

Sous vide is a cooking method where food is encased in special plastic bags with all the air removed, then gently cooked in water. This method is easily accomplished in the Ninja® Foodi® SmartLid™.

### Slow Cook

The Ninja® Foodi® SmartLid™ is also a slow cooker! Let food cook all day in this appliance and come home to fabulous meals ready and waiting for you.

### Yogurt

Did you know you can even make yogurt in this appliance? Milk and a starter are kept at the perfect temperature so you can have your own homemade yogurt anytime.

## OPERATING BUTTONS

Now that you understand the SmartLid Slider™ on the SmartLid™ and the functions it controls, let's take a look at the Operating Buttons that you will use to customize the Ninja® Foodi® SmartLid™ for each recipe. These buttons operate independently of the SmartLid Slider™.

Some versions of the SmartLid™ have a probe attached, which will help ensure accuracy in cooking and reaching safe final internal temperatures for large pieces of meat. But the 6-in-1 model has everything you need.

### Temp

To set the temperature, press Temp and then turn the Start/Stop dial to select the temperature according to the recipe you are making. You can adjust the temperature in 5ºF increments. This button is also used to adjust the pressure level when pressure cooking.

### Start/Stop

This dial lets you choose a cooking function, cook temperature, and cook time. Press the button to start cooking. If you press this button while the unit is working, it will stop the current cooking function.

### Function Dial

This dial lets you choose a cooking function: Air fry, bake, bread, broil, roast, dehydrate, proof, reheat, sear/sauté, steam, sous vide, slow cook, and yogurt. These functions can be used without the crisp capability.

### Time

Press the Time button and then rotate the Start/Stop button to adjust the cooking time for each recipe. You can adjust the time while the machine is cooking by pressing the button and then using the Start/Stop dial to change it.

### Keep Warm

After pressure cooking, slow cooking, or steaming, the Ninja® Foodi® SmartLid™ will automatically switch to Keep Warm mode and the timer will start counting up. Keep Warm will stay on for 12 hours, or you may press the button to turn it off.

### Power

The power button turns the Ninja® Foodi® SmartLid™ on and off and stops all cooking functions with one touch.

## SPOTLIGHT ON STEAM & CRISP MEALS

The Steam & Crisp function sets the Ninja® Foodi® SmartLid™ apart from other multicookers on the market. The ease in preparation, cooking, and cleanup will have you turning to this appliance again and again during the week. Using the Deluxe Reversible Rack, you can stack different types of foods to cook at the same time. Add a grain to the lower level, place vegetables of your choice over it, and then add a protein on top. This creates a meal in one pot. For instance, make Honey Mustard Chicken Thighs, Garlic Green Beans, and Rice Pilaf (page 140), choose a Broccoli-Cheddar Frittata (page 44), or make Barbecue Marinated Steak Tips with Corn on the Cob and Yellow Rice (page 176). Or you can experiment with your own choices when you have made some recipes and feel more comfortable with the appliance.

## Bakery-Quality Bread Without Using the Oven

The Ninja® Foodi® SmartLid™ bakes great flavorful bread with a thick, crispy, and chewy crust thanks to the Steam and Crisp functions. Most people don't know that steam is the secret to the best bread. Steam works throughout the baking process to create the perfect loaf. At first, the steam keeps the dough soft so the dough can rise more while in the oven (this is called oven spring). The extra moisture also slows down the cooking process so the bread bakes evenly. Steam also dissolves sugars on the surface of the dough, enabling them to combine with proteins to create that beautiful brown color, known as nonenzymatic browning. As the bread bakes, moisture on the surface of the dough from the steam creates a gel from the starches in the flour, which makes a crisp and crackly crust as the bread dries. The moisture also absorbs some of the heat of the oven, which prevents the gluten in the flour from denaturing too quickly, so the dough stays softer and more flexible as it bakes for a tender crumb. You'll find that breads are so much more delicious when baked in the Ninja® Foodi® SmartLid™.

# SMARTLID™ FAQ

**Q:** **How do I convert my favorite recipes to the Ninja®**
**Foodi® SmartLid™?**
To convert conventional oven recipes to the Ninja® Foodi®
SmartLid™, use the Bake/Roast function, reduce the temperature by
25°F, and reference the charts on page 218 for proper cooking time.
For cakes, use the Steam & Bake function, reduce the box temperature by 40°F, and reduce the box cook time by 20 minutes. For quick
breads, use the Steam & Bake function, reduce the box temperature
by 50°F, and reduce the box cook time by 20 minutes.

**Q:** **Can I swap ingredients in recipes?**
We suggest keeping to the ingredients the recipes call for, as the
cooking times and temperatures vary based on the ingredients.
However, substitutes can be pulled from the Steam Air Fry Charts on
page 218. Be sure to adjust the cooking time and temperature accord-
ingly for the best output.

**Q:** **What is the different between Steam & Crisp and Air Fry?**
Steam & Crisp keeps foods juicy on the inside while crisping the
outside at the same time. It is best for whole roasts, fresh and frozen
proteins, root vegetables, and creating multitiered, whole meals. Air
Fry cooks foods to crunchy perfection. It is best for frozen prepared
food like chicken nuggets, frozen fries, and mozzarella sticks.

**Q:** **What is the difference between Steam & Bake and Bake?**
Steam & Bake is best used for foods you want to become fluffy and
moist, such as cakes and cupcakes. Bake is best for dense baked good
that should become rich and gooey, like cookies and brownies.

# 2

# Start Cooking with Your SmartLid™!

**NOW THAT YOU UNDERSTAND HOW THE NINJA® FOODI®** SmartLid™ works, let's turn to the recipes. You will be amazed at the variety of foods that can be prepared in this versatile appliance. You can make quick breads, egg dishes for breakfast, roasts, pastries, chicken wings, jerky and fruit leathers, roasted vegetables, and entire meals. Some of the recipes in this book include Mediterranean Halibut en Papillote-ish (page 118), Chicken Fajitas (page 142), Teriyaki Tofu with Ginger White Rice and Mushrooms (page 87), Twice-Baked Cheddar Broccoli Potatoes (page 97), Spiced Grilled Chicken with Pilau Rice (page 153), Beef Wellington (page 178), Shepherd's Pie (page 174), Garlic Dinner Rolls (page 201), Key Lime Cheesecake with Mango Sauce (page 192), Chocolate Chip Zucchini Bread (page 199), Fish and Chips (page 114), and much, much more.

# READY, SET, CRISP!

One of the best things about the SmartLid™ is that you don't need fancy ingredients in order to cook amazing meals. Still, there are some ingredients you really do need to have on hand. These ingredients are pantry, refrigerator, and freezer staples that will help you get the most out of this wonderful and versatile appliance. All are readily available in most grocery stores, none are unusual or expensive, and your family will love all of them. Let's go through these foods one at a time.

## Simple Staples

You probably already have lots of these ingredients on hand. It's a good idea to devise a system that will help you keep track of these foods and replenish them when your supply gets low.

**Bread crumbs.** Dried bread crumbs, along with a special type of crisp crumb called panko, are used to create crisp coatings on meats and poultry.

**Butter.** Butter is used in baking and to make sauces, as well as to add flavor and to sauté vegetables and meats. Most recipes in this book use unsalted butter.

**Canned tomato products.** Many soup, stew, and sauce recipes use canned tomatoes. Stock whole tomatoes, tomato sauce and paste, and diced tomatoes in juice.

**Cheese.** Your favorite cheeses should be on hand all the time. Choose cheddar, Swiss, Parmesan, and specialty cheeses such as pepper Jack.

**Chicken and beef stock.** These essential ingredients are used to make soups, stews, and sauces and are used in marinades as well.

**Eggs.** Eggs make great breakfasts, and they are used in baked goods to provide structure. They are also used to coat meats for crisp crusts. Buy large AA grade eggs.

**Fish and seafood.** Fresh and frozen fish and seafood make wonderful meals. Stock fish fillets, shrimp, and salmon fillets.

**Flour and baking ingredients.** Use all-purpose flour to make baked goods such as cakes and cookies and piecrusts, and to coat meats before sautéing for a crisp crust. Baking powder, baking soda, and yeast are used to make breads and cakes.

**Fresh vegetables and fruit.** You'll need onions, garlic, carrots, potatoes, mushrooms, broccoli, green beans, and other vegetables your family enjoys. Apples, bananas, and strawberries are other good staple fruit choices.

**Meat and poultry.** Fresh and frozen meats and poultry should be in your refrigerator and freezer. Choose ground beef, roasts, pork chops, whole chickens, and chicken parts.

**Milk and dairy products.** Milk is used to make sauces and in recipes such as cakes and cookies. You can choose from whole-milk or low-fat varieties, and you can use nondairy milks as well. Also, stock yogurt, sour cream, and heavy (whipping) cream.

**Oil, extra-virgin olive, and canola.** These oils are used to sauté vegetables and brown meats and are also used in salad dressings and baking.

**Pasta.** There are so many different types of pasta to choose from. Stock ziti, macaroni, spaghetti, and ramen, along with your family's favorites.

**Rice and whole grains.** Rice cooks beautifully in the Ninja® Foodi® SmartLid™. It's a staple in many cuisines and adds interest to meals. Keep brown rice, white rice, and wild rice on hand. Also stock quinoa and barley.

**Sugar.** You need sugar to make baked goods such as cookies, cakes, and muffins. It's also used in sauces and dressings. Stock granulated sugar, brown sugar, and powdered sugar.

## Keep It Spicy

**Basil.** This herb has a sweet and lemony scent and is used in Italian cuisine. It pairs beautifully with vegetables and chicken.

**Chili powder.** A combination of spices such as dried chiles, paprika, garlic and onion powder, cayenne pepper, and sometimes cinnamon is used in Mexican cooking to add a punch of flavor.

**Cinnamon.** This spice, which is actually the bark of a special tree species, adds great flavor and aroma to baked goods and is used in some ethnic cuisines as well. Stock ground cinnamon and whole cinnamon sticks.

**Curry powder.** Indian cuisine uses curry powder, another spice blend, to add intense flavor to foods. Curry powder contains paprika, turmeric, chiles, dried mustard, and peppers.

**Herbs and spices.** Herbs and spices add flavor to food and are essential staples. Buy dried varieties in small quantities in sealed jars and cans because they will keep their flavor no longer than a year. Mark the date of purchase on each container. Fresh herbs last only a few days in the refrigerator.

**Italian seasoning.** This is another blend of dried herbs used in Italian recipes such as spaghetti sauce and lasagna. Italian seasoning is a combination of dried oregano, basil, and thyme.

**Onion powder and garlic powder.** The dried, powdered forms of these root vegetables are used in sauces, soups, and stews when the fresh variety is too intrusive.

**Oregano.** Oregano is a spicy herb used in Italian recipes. It is delicious with beef and hearty root vegetables.

**Paprika.** Paprika is used to color foods and sauces and to provide a warm, mellow spiciness. You can buy sweet and hot paprika depending on your tastes.

**Salt and pepper.** Every recipe calls for these flavor enhancers. The recipes in this book generally use kosher salt. Buy whole black peppercorns to put into a pepper grinder.

**Thyme.** This herb has a delicate lemony aroma and taste. Thyme is used in chicken recipes and in soups and stews.

## COOK ANYTHING IN YOUR SMARTLID™

If you don't have the ingredients on hand to make a specific recipe, don't worry! The charts beginning on page 20 will help you use the foods currently in your pantry, refrigerator, and freezer to make delicious recipes and complete flavorful meals in minutes. These simple combinations make satisfying dishes your family will love. And everything will be cooked to perfection.

# MAKE A STEAM & CRISP MEAL WITH PASTA

## 1. Start with the bottom layer

Add grain, water, and additional ingredients per box directions.

## 2. Assemble middle layer

Cover the bottom layer of the Deluxe Reversible Rack with aluminum foil. Place the rack in the pot. Place prepared vegetables on top of the aluminum foil.

| PASTA<br>12–16-oz box | SAUCE | VEGETABLE<br>2 cups mix & match. Coat with 1 tbsp oil and season. |
|---|---|---|
| White pasta, uncooked | **Tomato sauce**<br>2 (24-oz each) jars marinara sauce<br>3 cups chicken or vegetable stock | 1 pint cherry tomatoes |
| | **Creamy alfredo**<br>1 (16-oz) jar alfredo sauce<br>3 cups chicken stock<br>1 cup whole milk | 3 zucchini, cut in half lengthwise |
| Whole-wheat pasta, uncooked | **Stock (plain pasta)**<br>4 cups chicken or vegetable | 1 head (10 oz) broccoli, cut in half |
| | | 3 bell peppers, cut in 1-inch strips |
| Gluten-free pasta, uncooked | **Blush sauce**<br>2 (24-oz) jars marinara sauce<br>2½ cups chicken or vegetable stock<br>½ cup heavy cream | 10 oz cauliflower florets |
| | **Water (sauceless)**<br>4 cups | 1 bunch asparagus, trimmed |

**Too much pasta?** Cut the sauces in half with 8 oz of pasta: **Tomato Sauce:** 1 jar (24 oz) marinara sauce, 2 cups chicken stock; **Creamy Alfredo:** 1½ cups chicken stock, 1 cup whole milk, 1 jar (15-oz ) alfredo sauce, ½ cup grated Parmesan cheese (stir in to thicken sauce after cooking is complete)

# 3. Assemble top layer

Select a protein and season as desired. Slide the Deluxe Layer through the lower layer's handles. Place the protein on the top layer of the rack. Close lid, move slider to STEAMCRISP, and select STEAM & CRISP. Set time and temperature based on protein. Add finishing touches as desired.

| PROTEIN<br>Fresh and frozen | SEASON* | CRISPING TEMPERATURE & TIME |
|---|---|---|
| 4 chicken breasts, boneless, skinless (6-8 oz each) | | 390°F for 10-15 minutes |
| 6 Italian sausages | | 390°F for 8-10 minutes |
| 12 plant-based meatballs (fresh or frozen) | Italian seasoning<br><br>Herbs de Provence | 425°F for 5-10 minutes |
| 6 plant-based sausages | Lemon pepper seasoning | |
| 6 portobella mushroom caps, 6 (3 inches each) or 3 (4 inches each) | Seasoning salt | 450°F for 5-10 minutes |
| 4 frozen chicken breasts, boneless skinless (6-8 oz each) | Garlic and herb seasoning<br><br>Seasoning of choice | 375°F for 10-15 minutes |
| 4 frozen breaded eggplant cutlets | | 450°F for 8-10 minutes |
| 4 frozen breaded chicken breast cutlets (5 oz each) | | 450°F for 7-10 minutes |
| 12 frozen meatballs | TIP:<br>Marinate proteins up to 6 hours or buy them pre-marinated to save time. | 375°F for 10-15 minutes |
| 6 frozen plant-based sausages | | 400°F for 5-10 minutes |
| 12 frozen jumbo shrimp | | 425°F for 2-5 minutes |

*For thicker cuts of meat, add 2-3 minutes to cook time. Note that in doing this you may run the risk of overcooking the other meal components, so we recommend keeping meat thickness within the given guidelines.

**Finishing touches:** When cooking is complete, add finishing touches by stirring cheese, spinach, arugula, or pesto into the pasta.

# MAKE A STEAM & CRISP MEAL WITH GRAINS

## 1. Start with the bottom layer

Add grain, water, and additional ingredients per box directions.

## 2. Assemble middle layer

Cover the bottom layer of the Deluxe Reversible Rack with aluminum foil. Place the rack in the pot. Place prepared vegetables on top of the aluminum foil.

| GRAIN | VEGETABLE<br>2 cups mix & match. Coat with 1 tbsp oil and season. |
|---|---|
| 2 cup white rice, rinsed<br>4 cups water or stock<br>2 tablespoons butter or oil | 1 lb sweet potatoes, cut in 1-inch pieces |
| 2 cups quinoa, rinsed<br>3 cups water or stock | 1 lb baby potatoes, cut in half |
| 2 cups Israeli couscous<br>3 cups water or stock<br>1 tablespoon butter or oil | 1 bunch asparagus, trimmed |
| | 10 oz cauliflower florets |
| 1 cup Arborio rice<br>4 cups water or stock | 3 zucchini, cut in half lengthwise |
| | 24 oz butternut squash, cut in cubes |
| 1 cup instant brown rice<br>2 cups water or stock | 1 head (10 oz) broccoli, cut in half |
| | 3 parsnips, cut in 1-inch pieces |
| Rice and beans, boxed<br>Cajun-style rice, boxed<br>Spanish-style rice, boxed<br>Rice pilaf, boxed<br>Add water, seasoning,<br>and oil per box instructions | 2 small onions, peeled, cut in quarters |
| | 3 bell peppers, cut in 1-inch strips |

## 3. Assemble top layer

Select a protein and season as desired. Slide the Deluxe Layer through the lower layer's handles. Place protein on the top layer of the rack. Close lid, move slider to STEAMCRISP, and select STEAM & CRISP. Set time and temperature based on protein. Add finishing touches as desired.

| PROTEIN<br>Fresh and frozen | SEASON* | CRISPING TEMPERATURE & TIME |
|---|---|---|
| 4 chicken breasts, boneless, skinless (6–8 oz each) | | 390°F for 10–15 minutes |
| 6 Italian sausages | BBQ seasoning | 390°F for 8–10 minutes |
| 1 (8-oz) package seitan, cut in 1-inch pieces | Jerk seasoning | |
| 6 plant-based sausages | Seasoning salt | |
| 1 (8-oz) package tempeh cut in ¼-inch strips or 1-inch cubes | Garlic and herb seasoning | 425°F for 5–10 minutes |
| | Fajita seasoning | |
| 6 portobella mushroom caps, 6 (3 inches each) or 3 (4 inches each) | Seasoning of choice | 450°F for 5–10 minutes |
| 4 frozen chicken breasts, boneless skinless (6–8 oz each) | | 375°F for 10–15 minutes |
| 4 frozen breaded eggplant cutlets | **TIP:**<br>Marinate proteins up to 6 hours or buy them pre-marinated to save time. | 450°F for 8–10 minutes |
| 4 frozen breaded chicken breast cutlets (5 oz each) | | 450°F for 7–10 minutes |
| 12 frozen meatballs | | 375°F for 10–15 minutes |
| 6 frozen plant-based sausages | | 400°F for 5–10 minutes |
| 12 frozen jumbo shrimp | | 425°F for 2–5 minutes |

**Finishing touches:** When cooking is complete, add finishing touches by stirring cheese, spinach, arugula, or pesto into the grains.

# 6 TIPS FOR COOKING IN YOUR SMARTLID™

The Ninja® Foodi® SmartLid™ is seamless to use, of course, but these tips will help you get the most out of the appliance.

**Season food before cooking.** Season your food with salt, pepper, spices, and herbs before it goes into the appliance. Salt especially is crucial because it will season every layer and enhance the natural flavors of the food.

**Put food in a single layer in the basket.** When arranging food in the Cook & Crisp™ Basket, arrange it in a single layer so the hot air can reach every piece. If you don't do this, parts of the food will not crisp and brown properly.

**Stir food halfway through air frying.** During air frying, you will most likely have to stir or rearrange the food so it cooks evenly. Use silicone-tipped tongs or a heatproof spatula to move the food around.

**When using the pressure cooker, leave the food alone.** Let the pressure cooker work without disturbing the appliance or the food. It takes time for pressure to build up to cook the food safely, and you don't want to disturb that equilibrium.

**Prep food according to the recipe instructions.** If the recipe tells you to slice or cube food to about the same size, follow those directions so the food cooks evenly and at the same time.

**Don't add too much oil.** The best part about air frying is that you only need a little bit of oil for super crisp and brown results. Don't add too much oil before adding the food to the appliance.

## ABOUT THE RECIPES

The delicious and easy recipes in this book cover every category and course. You will find great choices for breakfast, snacks, side dishes, main dishes, and desserts. Many recipes are for complete meals. Some of the recipes offer substitutions and variations so you can adapt the recipes to use what you like or what you have on hand.

Each recipe comes with complete nutritional information to help you make healthy choices. And each recipe will have a label that identifies which are appropriate for food allergies and preferences. For instance, a recipe for a customizable frittata lets you make breakfast no matter what your family's likes or dislikes. Make Mac and Pimento Cheese Bites (page 70) for a teenager's party. Choose Barbecue Cauliflower Tacos with Cabbage Slaw and Avocado (page 80) or Carne Asada Tacos (page 185) for a fun family Tex-Mex night. Make Fish and Chips (page 114) for a weekday meal, or Chicken Parm with Pasta Primavera (page 155) or Beef Wellington (page 178) for weekend entertaining. And finish your meal with Orange Upside-Down Olive Oil Cake (page 194) or Chocolate Chip Zucchini Bread (page 199).

### Labels

**Dairy-Free:** Recipes made without dairy, including milk, cheeses, sour cream, and yogurt.

**Gluten-Free:** These recipes are made without ingredients that contain gluten, including flour, bread, crackers, bulgur, barley, rye, and some types of oats.

**Nut-Free:** These recipes are appropriate for people with nut allergies. The recipes omit tree nuts, peanuts, and coconut.

**SteamCrisp Meals:** A true one-pot meal that includes a protein, vegetable, and/or starch.

**Vegan:** Vegan recipes are made with plant-based foods and without any animal products such as meat, poultry, and fish. The recipes also omit foods made from animal products, including honey, granulated sugar that is purified with bone char, cheese, and dairy.

**Vegetarian:** Vegetarian foods are made without meat, fish, and poultry. They may include eggs, cheese, and dairy products.

## Time

Each recipe breaks down the total time required from start to finish, step by step. The time required to steam and proof breads, or to build pressure and pressure release for pressure cooking, plus sautéing and searing foods, are all spelled out so you can plan and time your meals every night.

## Accessories

Most recipes use one of the accessories described earlier in this book. You will know exactly what you need to make each recipe, such as the Multi-Purpose Pan, Deluxe Reversible Rack, or the Cook & Crisp™ Basket, in addition to spatulas, spoons, and knives.

Now let's start cooking! Read through the recipes and choose the ones you want to make. Check to see which ingredients you have on hand and the ones you will need to purchase, then shop. Make sure you understand how each recipe works and how to use the Ninja® Foodi® SmartLid™ for each step. Let the machine do all the work, then relax and enjoy eating your delicious creations.

**Banana Berry Parfait with Homemade Yogurt and Granola,** *page 32*

# 3

# Breakfast

# Blueberry Baked Oatmeal

**SERVES 6 TO 8**

*Baked oatmeal is a great way to change up breakfast from plain old everyday oatmeal. Using the Ninja® Foodi® SmartLid™ and its new SteamCrisp™ technology, you can create a healthy and delicious breakfast in no time! Using the Steam & Crisp function ensures the oats cook all the way through while creating the perfect crunchy topping to contrast with the creamy oats. Juicy blueberries and crunchy pecans round out this recipe for a delicious breakfast or snack.*
—by Melissa Celli

**VEGETARIAN**

**Prep Time:** 5 minutes
**Total Cook Time:**
35 minutes
**Steam:** about 15 minutes
**Cook:** 20 minutes

2 cups old-fashioned oats

1 teaspoon baking powder

½ teaspoon kosher salt

2 teaspoons pumpkin
   pie seasoning

½ cup brown sugar, divided

¾ cup pecan
   halves, divided

2 tablespoons maple syrup

1 cup whole milk

1 teaspoon vanilla extract

¾ cup water

½ stick (4 tablespoons)
   unsalted butter, melted

2 large eggs, beaten

1 pint fresh
   blueberries, divided

Greek yogurt or
   whipped cream, for
   topping (optional)

1. In a large bowl, combine the oats, baking powder, salt, pumpkin pie seasoning, ¼ cup of brown sugar, and half the pecans. Stir until evenly combined.

2. In a separate large bowl, whisk together the maple syrup, milk, vanilla, water, butter, and eggs until evenly combined.

3. Place half of the oat mixture in the pot. Sprinkle with half of the blueberries, then top with the remaining oat mixture.

**4.** Drizzle the maple syrup mixture over the oat mixture in the pot. Top with the remaining ¼ cup of brown sugar and remaining blueberries and pecans.

**5.** Close the lid and move the slider to STEAMCRISP. Select STEAM & CRISP, set the temperature to 350°F, and set the time to 20 minutes. Press START/STOP to begin cooking (PrE will display for about 15 minutes as the unit steams, then the timer will start counting down).

**6.** When cooking is complete, spoon the oatmeal into bowls and serve warm with Greek yogurt (if using).

**Per serving:** *Calories: 448; Total Fat: 22g; Saturated Fat: 7g; Cholesterol: 86mg; Sodium: 207mg; Carbohydrates: 55g; Fiber: 6g; Protein: 11g*

**Substitution Tip:**
Replace the milk in the recipe with your favorite nondairy milk and the butter with a nondairy variety to enjoy this oatmeal as a dairy-free breakfast or snack.

# Banana Berry Parfait with Homemade Yogurt and Granola

**SERVES 4 TO 6**

*If you've never made your own homemade yogurt, you're in for a treat. The Ninja® Foodi® SmartLid™ makes every step easier. With just the simplest ingredients, you can have an amazing breakfast, snack, or even dessert. Store-bought yogurt is great strictly for the convenience, but when you make yogurt from scratch in your unit, you will never want to go back to buying it. One of the greatest things about this treat is that the possibilities are endless: You can add all kinds of toppings, such as fruit or your favorite jam.* —by Myles Bryan

**NUT-FREE**
**VEGETARIAN**

**Prep Time:** 5 minutes, plus 4 hours to chill
**Total Cook Time:** 8 hours 15 minutes
**Cook:** 8 hours
**Bake:** 15 minutes

**FOR THE YOGURT**
½ **gallon whole milk**
3 **tablespoons plain yogurt with active live cultures**
1 **tablespoon vanilla extract (optional)**
½ **cup honey (optional)**

**FOR THE GRANOLA**
½ **cup extra-virgin olive oil**
½ **cup maple syrup**
1 **teaspoon ground cinnamon**
1 **teaspoon kosher salt**
3 **cups old-fashioned rolled oats**
1 **cup raw pumpkin seeds**
1 **cup raisins**

**TOPPINGS**
4 **strawberries, sliced**
1 **banana, sliced**
½ **cup blueberries**

1. **To make the yogurt:** Pour the milk into the pot. Make sure the pressure release valve is in the VENT position (this aids the milk cooking low and slow). Close the lid and move the slider to AIR FRY/STOVETOP. Select YOGURT and set the time to 8 hours. Press START/STOP to begin.

**2.** After the milk has boiled, the display will read "Cool." Note that this process can take several hours. Once cooled, the unit will beep and display "Add & Stir." Allow the pressure to release naturally. Open the lid and skim the skin off the top of the milk and discard. Allow the milk to cool, stirring frequently, for about 5 minutes.

**3.** Add the yogurt to the pot and whisk until fully incorporated. Press START/STOP to continue cooking.

**4.** After 8 hours, transfer the yogurt to a glass container and chill for a minimum of 4 hours in the refrigerator.

**5. To make the granola:** While the yogurt chills, wipe the pot clean. In a large bowl, combine the olive oil, maple syrup, cinnamon, kosher salt, oats, pumpkin seeds, and raisins, then transfer to the pot.

**6.** Close the lid and move the slider to AIR FRY/ STOVETOP. Select BAKE/ROAST, set the temperature to 300°F, and set the time to 15 minutes (if a crunchier granola is desired, add 5 more minutes). Press START/ STOP to begin cooking.

**7.** When cooking is complete, open the lid and let the granola cool for at least 15 minutes.

**8.** Once the yogurt is chilled, add the vanilla and honey (if using). Serve with granola and the strawberries, banana, and blueberries.

**Hack It:** Store extra yogurt in an airtight container in the refrigerator for up to 2 weeks.

**Per serving:** *Calories: 830; Total Fat: 46g; Saturated Fat: 14g; Cholesterol: 49mg; Sodium: 462mg; Carbohydrates: 94g; Fiber: 9g; Protein: 28g*

# Cinnamon Pecan Buns

**MAKES 8 BUNS**

*These buns are fluffy, sticky in all the right ways, and enjoyable at any hour of the day. With just a little patience while the buns proof twice at exactly the right temperature in the Ninja® Foodi® SmartLid™, you're rewarded with a magnificent yeasty flavor. Although these buns are like traditional cinnamon rolls, they're instead baked on top of a bed of caramelized sugar and pecans, giving them a nutty buttery coating that will truly elevate every brunch or special occasion. You can use dark or light brown sugar interchangeably in this recipe.* —by Avery Lowe

**VEGETARIAN**

**Prep Time:** 15 minutes
**Proof:** 40 minutes
(first rise) + 25 minutes
(second rise)
**Total Cook Time:**
25 minutes
**Steam:** about 5 minutes
**Bake:** 20 minutes

**Accessories:** Ninja®
Multi-Purpose Pan or
8-inch round baking pan,
Deluxe Reversible Rack
(bottom layer only)

Nonstick cooking spray

3 tablespoons
granulated sugar

1 cup whole milk, warmed

1 (0.25-ounce) envelope
active dry yeast

12 tablespoons (1½ sticks)
unsalted butter, at room
temperature, divided

2 large eggs, beaten

1 teaspoon kosher
salt, divided

3 cups all-purpose flour,
plus more as needed

1¼ cups brown
sugar, divided

3 tablespoons ground
cinnamon

1 cup pecans,
finely chopped

½ cup water, for steaming

1 cup powdered sugar

2 tablespoons whole milk

1. Spray the Multi-Purpose Pan with cooking spray.

2. In a large bowl, whisk together the granulated sugar, the milk, and the yeast. Let the yeast foam for about 5 minutes.

3. After 5 minutes, add 3 tablespoons of butter, the eggs, ½ teaspoon of salt, and the flour, 1 cup at a time. Stir until the dough comes together.

4. Lightly dust a clean work surface with flour. Turn out the dough onto the surface and knead it for 5 minutes into a smooth ball. If the dough is sticky, add flour 1 tablespoon at a time to prevent sticking.

*CONTINUED >*

**5.** Place the dough ball in the prepared pan. Place the pan on the bottom layer of the Deluxe Reversible Rack in the lower position, then place the rack in the pot.

**6.** Close the lid and move the slider to AIR FRY/ STOVETOP. Select PROOF, set the temperature to 80ºF, and set the time to 40 minutes. Press START/STOP to begin the first rise.

**7.** While the dough is proofing, make the filling. Combine 5 tablespoons of butter, ¾ cup of brown sugar, the cinnamon, and the remaining ½ teaspoon of salt in a small bowl and stir well. Set aside.

**8.** In a medium bowl, combine 3 tablespoons of butter and the remaining ½ cup of brown sugar and stir. Set aside.

**9.** When the rise is complete, dust a flat, clean work surface with flour. Remove the dough from the pot and place it on the work surface. Roll the dough into a 12-by-12-inch square and brush with the remaining 1 tablespoon of butter. Then, sprinkle with the cinnamon-sugar filling mixture, leaving a 1-inch border on all sides. Roll the dough into a log and slice it into 8 equal pieces.

**10.** Place the brown sugar and butter mixture in the pan and spread it into an even layer. Top with the pecans. Place the dough pieces close together, cut-side up, in the pan on top of the pecans. Gently press the buns to make them the same height.

**11.** Pour the water into the pot. Place the pan on the bottom layer of the Deluxe Reversible Rack in the lower position, then place the rack in the pot.

**12.** Close the lid. Select PROOF, set the temperature to 80ºF, and set the time to 25 minutes. Press START/STOP to begin the second rise.

**13.** After 25 minutes, move the slider to STEAMCRISP, select STEAM & BAKE, set the temperature to 300ºF, and set the time to 20 minutes. Select START/STOP to begin cooking (PrE will display for about 5 minutes as the unit steams, then the timer will start counting down).

**14.** While the cinnamon buns are cooking, prepare the glaze. In a small bowl, whisk together the powdered sugar and milk until well combined.

**15.** When cooking is complete, remove the rack with the pan. Let the buns cool for 10 minutes in the pan, then flip the pan over a plate to release the buns. Drizzle with the glaze and serve warm.

*Per serving (1 bun): Calories: 746; Total Fat: 30g; Saturated Fat: 13g; Cholesterol: 96mg; Sodium: 192mg; Carbohydrates: 114 g; Fiber: 4g; Protein: 9g*

**Substitution Tip:** Don't have pecans? Substitute walnut halves and pieces.

# Cuban-Style Ham and Cheese Breakfast Pastry

**SERVES 4**

*There is a Cuban bakery in San Diego called Azúcar that was just a few blocks from our home in Ocean Beach. I can't tell you how many times we walked down there for breakfast, lunch, or dessert, buying their mini cakes and delicious breakfast pastries. We remain loyal to Azúcar despite now being 3,000 miles away! Though I can't recreate the experience of walking down Newport Ave. with a guava cheese danish, I've put together traditional Cuban flavors and made these pastries quick and easy to enjoy.* —by Kara Bleday

**NUT-FREE**

**Prep Time:** 5 minutes
**Total Cook Time:**
35 minutes
**Steam:** about 20 minutes
**Bake:** 15 minutes

**Accessories:** Ninja®
Multi-Purpose Pan or
8-inch round baking pan,
Deluxe Reversible Rack
(bottom layer only)

½ cup water, for steaming

1⅓ sheets frozen puff pastry dough (about 9¾-by-10½-inch), thawed, divided

6 slices Havarti cheese, halved

6 slices deli ham

½ cup sliced pickles

1 tablespoon Dijon mustard

1. Pour the water into the pot.

2. Cut the puff pastry into 4 equal rectangles (if the pastry has perforated lines, use those as a guide). Lay the sheets in stacks of two side by side. Using the Multi-Purpose Pan as a template, place the pan over the stacks of puff pastry and cut to size. Discard any excess dough. You will have 4 circles when complete.

3. Place the bottom layers of puff pastry in the pan. Top with 3 slices of Havarti cheese, the ham, then the remaining 3 slices of cheese, and the pickles. Evenly spread the mustard on the remaining top pieces of puff pastry, then place them mustard-side down on top of the filling in the pan to close the sandwiches. The top pieces of pastry just sit on top; the edges do not need to be sealed.

**4.** Place the pan on the bottom layer of the Deluxe Reversible Rack in the lower position, then place the rack in the pot.

**5.** Close the lid and move the slider to STEAMCRISP. Select STEAM & BAKE, set the temperature to 350°F, and set the time to 15 minutes. Press START/STOP to begin cooking (PrE will display for about 20 minutes as the unit steams, then the timer will start counting down).

**6.** When cooking is complete, remove the rack with the pan. Allow the pastry to cool for 10 minutes before cutting each pastry in half to serve.

*Per serving:* *Calories: 662; Total Fat: 46g; Saturated Fat: 16g; Cholesterol: 60mg; Sodium: 1144mg; Carbohydrates: 38g; Fiber: 2g; Protein: 25g*

**Substitution Tip:** To make this vegetarian, substitute leftover roasted vegetables for the ham and enjoy a bright breakfast pastry.

# Breakfast Calzones

*Did you know that SteamCrisp™ technology is the perfect cooking environment for doughs? Moisture-infused air plus convection work together to yield that perfect shiny crust with a tender, chewy interior that you'd find at your favorite bakery or pizza parlor. This recipe uses store-bought pizza dough and precooked bacon for a quick and easy breakfast that tastes as good as takeout. Impress your friends and family any time of day with this tasty twist on an Italian favorite.* —by Kelly Gray

---

**NUT-FREE**

**Prep Time:** 10 minutes
**Proof:** 30 minutes
**Total Cook Time:** 40 minutes
**Sear/Sauté:** 5 minutes
**Steam:** about 5 minutes
**Cook:** 30 minutes

**Accessories:** Deluxe Reversible Rack (bottom layer only), Multi-Purpose Pan or 8-inch round baking pan, Cook & Crisp™ Basket

1 (16-ounce) package store-bought pizza dough, at room temperature, divided and rolled into 2 balls

All-purpose flour or canola oil, for rolling the dough

2 tablespoons whole milk

6 large eggs

Kosher salt

Freshly ground black pepper

1 tablespoon canola oil

4 strips cooked bacon, chopped

½ cup water, for steaming

½ cup tomato salsa

1½ cups shredded cheddar cheese

1. Place the Multi-Purpose Pan on the bottom layer of the Deluxe Reversible Rack in the lower position, then place the rack in the pot. Place the dough balls in the pan.

2. Close the lid and move the slider to AIR FRY/ STOVETOP. Select PROOF, set the temperature to 95°F, and set the time to 30 minutes. Press START/STOP to begin the rise.

3. When proofing is complete, carefully remove the rack and the pan. Place the dough balls on a clean, floured or oiled, work surface and roll into 8-inch round circles.

4. Select SEAR/SAUTÉ and set the temperature to 3. Select START/STOP to preheat the unit for 5 minutes.

CONTINUED >

**5.** While the unit is preheating, whisk together the milk and eggs in a small bowl. Season with salt and pepper.

**6.** Once the unit has preheated, pour the oil into the pot followed by the egg mixture. Allow the egg mixture to cook for about 2 minutes, stirring occasionally with a rubber spatula. Add the bacon and cook for 2 more minutes or until the eggs are almost set but still slightly runny.

**7.** Remove the eggs from the pot and set aside. Carefully wipe the pot clean and pour the water into the pot.

**8.** To assemble the calzones, put 2 tablespoons of salsa on half of each dough round, leaving a 1-inch perimeter. Add the egg mixture, cheese, and remaining 2 tablespoons of salsa.

**9.** Wet the edges of the dough with water and fold the dough over the toppings. Firmly press the edges of the dough to seal. Cut 3 vents on the top of each calzone.

**10.** Carefully transfer each calzone to the Cook & Crisp™ Basket with the flat sides touching in the center. Place the basket in the pot and close the lid.

**11.** Move the slider to STEAMCRISP. Select STEAM & CRISP, set the temperature to 340°F, and set the time to 30 minutes. Select START/STOP to begin (PrE will display for about 5 minutes as the unit steams, then the timer will start counting down).

**12.** When cooking is complete, remove the calzones and enjoy warm.

*Per serving: Calories: 1,288; Total Fat: 64g; Saturated Fat: 26g; Cholesterol: 663mg; Sodium: 2960mg; Carbohydrates: 113g; Fiber: 7g; Protein: 66g*

# Breakfast Potatoes

**SERVES 4**

*My favorite breakfast side is a breakfast potato. I especially love them when they are deep-fried—but I guess we can try to be a bit healthier and air fry them! These come out crispy on the outside and creamy on the inside with peppers and onions charred to perfection. It's so much easier than cooking on a stovetop or oven, and you really get a perfect crisp on every part of the potatoes.* —by Michelle Boland

DAIRY-FREE
GLUTEN-FREE
NUT-FREE
VEGAN

**Prep Time:** 10 minutes
**Total Cook Time:**
25 minutes
**Cook:** 25 minutes

**Accessories:** Cook & Crisp™ Basket

*Per serving: Calories: 213; Total Fat: 7g; Saturated Fat: 1g; Cholesterol: 0mg; Sodium: 52mg; Carbohydrates: 34g; Fiber: 5g; Protein: 4g*

½ cup water, for steaming
1½ pounds baby potatoes, halved
2 tablespoons extra-virgin olive oil
1 teaspoon paprika
1 teaspoon onion powder
1 teaspoon garlic powder
Kosher salt
Freshly ground black pepper
1 small yellow onion, diced
1 red bell pepper, diced

1. Pour the water into the pot.

2. In a medium bowl, combine the potatoes, oil, paprika, onion powder, and garlic powder. Season with salt and pepper and toss until combined and the potatoes are evenly coated.

3. Place the potatoes in the Cook & Crisp™ Basket and place the basket in the pot.

4. Close the lid and move the slider to AIR FRY/STOVETOP. Select AIR FRY, set the temperature to 450°F, and set the time to 25 minutes. Press START/STOP to begin cooking.

5. After 10 minutes, open the lid and add the onion and bell pepper to the potatoes. Toss to combine. Close the lid and continue cooking for another 10 minutes. After 10 minutes, open the lid and toss the potatoes. Close the lid and continue cooking for 5 minutes more.

6. When cooking is complete, carefully remove the basket from the pot and serve the potatoes immediately.

# Broccoli-Cheddar Frittata

**SERVES 6**

*Breakfast is one of my favorite meals of the day, and I'm always looking for ideas to prep ahead of time. I need something easy that is also good to transport when I'm heading to work in the Ninja® Test Kitchen. I love a frittata because not only does it last for the whole week, but I can also customize it with different ingredients. Broccoli-cheddar is my favorite combination, but you can get creative with your own favorites.* —by Meg Jordan

GLUTEN-FREE
NUT-FREE
VEGETARIAN

**Prep Time:** 10 minutes
**Total Cook Time:**
48 minutes
**Sear/Sauté:** 8 minutes
**Steam:** about 15 minutes
**Cook:** 25 minutes

**Accessories:** Ninja®
Multi-Purpose Pan or
8-inch round baking pan,
Deluxe Reversible Rack

- 3 tablespoons unsalted butter, plus more for greasing
- 1 medium yellow onion, diced
- Kosher salt
- Freshly ground black pepper
- 2 cups chopped broccoli florets
- 10 large eggs
- ½ cup whole milk
- 1½ cups shredded cheddar cheese
- 2 cups water, for steaming

1. Close the lid and move the slider to AIR FRY/STOVETOP. Select SEAR/SAUTÉ and set the temperature to 3. Open the lid and select START/STOP to begin preheating. Allow the unit to preheat for 5 minutes.

2. Put the butter in the pot. Once the butter has melted, add the onion and season with salt and pepper. Sauté for about 3 minutes or until the onion is translucent. Add the broccoli and stir, sautéing for another 3 minutes or until the broccoli is bright green and slightly softened.

3. Remove the onion and broccoli from the pot and set aside in a medium bowl. Wipe the pot clean.

4. In a large bowl, whisk together the eggs, milk, and more salt and pepper, if desired. Grease the Multi-Purpose Pan with butter.

**5.** Carefully fold the onion, broccoli, and cheddar cheese into the egg mixture, then pour the mixture into the prepared pan.

**6.** Pour the water into the pot. Place the pan on the bottom layer of the Deluxe Reversible Rack in the lower position, then place the rack in the pot.

**7.** Close the lid and move the slider to STEAMCRISP. Select STEAM & BAKE, set the temperature to 280ºF, and set the time to 25 minutes. Press START/STOP to begin cooking (PrE will display for about 15 minutes as the unit steams, then the timer will start counting down).

**8.** When cooking is complete, carefully remove the rack with the pan. Allow the frittata to cool for about 20 minutes, then serve, using a silicone-tipped utensil to slice the frittata.

**Per serving:** *Calories: 315; Total Fat: 24g; Saturated Fat: 12g; Cholesterol: 356mg; Sodium: 346mg; Carbohydrates: 6g; Fiber: 1g; Protein: 19g*

**Variation Tip:** Customize this frittata to make it your own with other filling ingredients, such as bacon or sautéed mushrooms.

# Upside-Down Ham and Cheese Quiche

*This recipe will turn your Sunday brunch upside down! What is upside-down quiche? It's quiche with the crust on top—think of a chicken potpie, but instead of chicken, veggies, and sauce as the filling, it's a delicate quiche with chunks of ham and melty cheese. This is a great recipe for entertaining because you can prep and cook the quiche ahead of time, freeing you up to be with your friends and family.*
—by Craig White

**NUT-FREE**

**Prep Time:** 10 minutes
**Total Cook Time:**
40 minutes
**Steam:** about 20 minutes
**Cook:** 20 minutes

**Accessories:** Ninja®
Multi-Purpose Pan or
8-inch round pan, Deluxe
Reversible Rack (bottom
layer only)

2 cups water, for steaming

Nonstick cooking spray

8 large eggs

¾ cup whole milk

¾ cup heavy
    (whipping) cream

1 cup shredded
    cheddar cheese

1 (8-ounce) boneless
    ham steak, diced

2 scallions, thinly sliced

Kosher salt

Freshly ground
    black pepper

1 (9-inch) ready-to-bake
    piecrust

**1.** Pour the water into the pot. Spray the Multi-Purpose Pan with cooking spray.

**2.** In a large bowl, whisk together the eggs, milk, and cream until combined. Add the cheese, ham, and scallions. Season with salt and pepper and stir to combine. Pour the mixture into the prepared pan.

**3.** Place the pie dough over the egg mixture in the pan and crimp the dough along the edges of the pan.

**4.** Place the pan on the bottom layer of the Deluxe Reversible Rack in the lower position, then place the rack in the pot. With the tip of a paring knife, poke about 50 holes in the dough.

**5.** Close the lid and move the slider to STEAMCRISP. Select STEAM & BAKE, set the temperature to 325ºF, and set the time to 20 minutes. Press START/STOP to begin cooking (PrE will display for about 20 minutes as the unit steams, then the timer will start counting down).

**6.** When cooking is complete, carefully remove the rack with the pan. Allow the quiche to cool and set for 20 minutes before serving directly from the pan.

**Per serving:** *Calories: 598; Total Fat: 42g; Saturated Fat: 17g; Cholesterol: 462mg; Sodium: 1316mg; Carbohydrates: 20g; Fiber: 1g; Protein: 34g*

**Variation Tip:** Quiche is a dish for using up leftovers. Try replacing the ham with cooked bacon or roasted broccoli.

# Shakshuka

**SERVES 2**

*Do you feel like something different for breakfast but don't think you have the time? Well, now you can make a delicious, healthy breakfast in about 20 minutes. With the Ninja® Foodi® SmartLid™ and its new SteamCrisp™ technology, you can have shakshuka in almost the same amount of time it would take to make scrambled eggs in a pan. This function uses steam and crisping to give you the perfect meal, without having to cook each item separately.* —by Jennie Vincent

DAIRY-FREE
GLUTEN-FREE
NUT-FREE
VEGETARIAN

**Prep Time:** 10 minutes
**Total Cook Time:**
16 minutes
**Sear/Sauté:** 6 minutes
**Steam:** about 5 minutes
**Cook:** 5 minutes

2 tablespoons
  extra-virgin olive oil

1 white onion, chopped

1 red bell pepper, seeded
  and chopped

1 garlic clove, minced

1 teaspoon ground cumin

½ teaspoon ground paprika

2 (14-ounce) cans
  diced tomatoes

Kosher salt

Freshly ground
  black pepper

4 large eggs

2 tablespoons chopped
  fresh cilantro

Bread, for serving
  (optional)

1. Close the lid and move the slider to AIR FRY/STOVETOP. Select SEAR/SAUTÉ and set the temperature to 4. Open the lid and select START/STOP to begin preheating. Preheat for 5 minutes.

2. After 5 minutes, pour the olive oil into the pot. Once hot, add the onion, bell pepper, and garlic and sauté until softened, about 3 minutes.

3. Add the cumin and paprika and sauté for 1 minute. Add the tomatoes and cook until warmed, about 2 minutes. Season with salt and pepper, then turn off the heat.

**4.** Create four wells in the vegetable mixture. Crack an egg into a small bowl, then carefully transfer it into one of the wells without breaking the yolk. Repeat with the remaining eggs.

**5.** Close the lid and move the slider to STEAMCRISP. Select STEAM & CRISP, set the temperature to 310°F, and set the time to 5 minutes. Press START/STOP to begin cooking (PrE will display for about 5 minutes as the unit steams, then the timer will start counting down).

**6.** When cooking is complete, sprinkle the shakshuka with the cilantro, season with salt and pepper, and serve immediately with bread (if using).

**Per serving:** *Calories: 374; Total Fat: 25g; Saturated Fat: 5g; Cholesterol: 372mg; Sodium: 684mg; Carbohydrates: 25g; Fiber: 10g; Protein: 17g*

**Variation Tip:** If you like more heat, just add a fresh chile or a little more paprika.

# Chilaquiles Verdes

**SERVES 6**

*This is a simplified and approachable adaptation of a Mexican dish traditionally made with freshly fried corn tortillas coated in flavorful homemade salsa that is simmered until the tortillas have softened. The mixture is often topped with an over-easy egg and garnished with options such as queso fresco, chopped onions, cilantro, and crema. In this version, we use premade salsa and chips to expedite the process a bit without compromising on flavor.* —by Kelly Gray

**NUT-FREE**

**Prep Time:** 10 minutes
**Total Cook Time:** 30 minutes
**Pressure Build:** about 10 minutes
**Pressure Cook:** 20 minutes
**Pressure Release:** Quick
**Bake:** 10 minutes

**Substitution Tip:** Don't like pork? Substitute boneless, skinless chicken thighs instead. The cooking time is the same, but you don't need to dice the chicken before cooking it.

- 2½ pounds boneless pork shoulder, cut into 2-inch pieces
- 2 (16-ounce) jars green salsa or green enchilada sauce
- 1½ cups chicken stock
- ½ cup chopped fresh cilantro, divided
- Kosher salt
- Freshly ground black pepper
- 1 (8- to 10-ounce) bag tortilla chips
- 6 large eggs
- ½ cup queso fresco, crumbled
- 1 cup prepared fresh pico de gallo

1. Put the pork shoulder, salsa, chicken stock, and ¼ cup of cilantro in the pot and stir until combined.

2. Close the lid and move the slider to PRESSURE. Make sure the pressure release valve is in the SEAL position. Select PRESSURE; the temperature will default to high, which is the correct setting. Set the time to 20 minutes and press START/STOP to begin cooking (the unit will build pressure for about 10 minutes before cooking begins).

3. When cooking is complete, select KEEP WARM and manually release the pressure. Move the slider to the AIR FRY/STOVETOP position, then carefully open the lid.

*CONTINUED >*

**Variation Tip:** Switch up the flavor by substituting red tomato salsa or enchilada sauce for the green.

4. Stir the contents of the pot and shred the pork using silicone-tipped tongs. Season with salt and pepper and add the tortilla chips to the pot. Stir until evenly combined.

5. Crack an egg into a small bowl, then carefully transfer it to the top of the pork mixture without breaking the yolk. Repeat with the remaining eggs.

6. Close the lid, select BAKE, set the temperature to 325°F, and set the time to 10 minutes. Select START/STOP to begin cooking.

7. When cooking is complete, open the lid. Serve warm and garnish with the remaining ¼ cup of cilantro, queso fresco, and pico de gallo.

**Per serving:** *Calories: 607; Total Fat: 23g; Saturated Fat: 6g; Cholesterol: 308mg; Sodium: 1028mg; Carbohydrates: 41g; Fiber: 4g; Protein: 56g*

**Charcuterie Board Bread,** *page 58*

# 4

# Snacks and Appetizers

# Mango-Habanero Chicken Jerky

**SERVES 4**

*For a twist on this road trip classic, chicken jerky is a leaner and more versatile alternative to beef. The key to making this jerky thin enough is freezing the chicken breasts and slicing from frozen. Once sliced and tossed in the marinade, this recipe is completely hands-off. After just a few hours in the dehydrator, you'll be ready to pack your bags and take this one on the road.* —by Avery Lowe

DAIRY-FREE
NUT-FREE

**Prep Time:** 15 minutes, plus 8 hours to marinate
**Total Cook Time:** 3 hours
**Dehydrate:** 3 hours

**Accessories:** Deluxe Reversible Rack (both layers)

**Hack It:** After you purchase the chicken breasts, take them out of their original packaging and wrap them tightly in plastic wrap. Let them freeze for a few hours or more. This will make the chicken easier to thinly slice (which is important to ensure the food-safety component of chicken jerky).

¾ **cup mango juice**

1 **cup canned pineapple chunks, juice drained**

4 **habanero chiles, seeded and diced**

1 **tablespoon honey**

1 **tablespoon apple cider vinegar**

2 **tablespoons soy sauce**

1 **tablespoon paprika**

2 **tablespoons canola oil**

1½ **tablespoons kosher salt**

1 **pound frozen boneless, skinless chicken breasts, cut into ¼-inch-thick slices**

1. In a large bowl, whisk together the mango juice, pineapple, habaneros, honey, vinegar, soy sauce, paprika, oil, and salt. Place the marinade and chicken in a large resealable plastic bag. Massage the outside of the bag to work the marinade over all parts of the chicken slices, then place the bag in the refrigerator for at least 8 hours and up to 24 hours to marinate.

2. Pour the chicken and marinade into a colander in the sink. Using tongs, push the chicken around to allow excess marinade to drain, then pat the chicken dry with paper towels.

**3.** Place the bottom layer of the Deluxe Reversible Rack in the lower position, then place the rack in the pot. Using the tongs, lay half the chicken slices flat on the rack, making sure none of the slices touch one another. Slide the Deluxe Layer through the lower layer's handles. Lay the remaining chicken flat on the top layer of the rack, again ensuring the slices don't touch.

**4.** Close the lid and move the slider to AIR FRY/STOVETOP. Select DEHYDRATE, set the temperature to 150°F, and set the time to 3 hours. Press START/STOP to begin cooking.

**5.** After 3 hours, check to see how the jerky is coming along. It should be thin, crisp, and cooked until no white meaty bits remain. If you would like your jerky cooked longer, cook in 30-minute intervals, checking after each interval, until it reaches your preference.

**6.** When cooking is complete, remove the rack layers with the jerky. Store the jerky in an airtight container at room temperature for up to 5 days or in the refrigerator for up to 2 weeks.

**Variation Tip:** To make the jerky spicier, double the amount of habanero chiles or add a tablespoon of your favorite hot sauce to the marinade. Regardless of how much habanero you use, be sure to wear gloves when prepping them. They are hot, hot, *hot*!

*Per serving: Calories: 182; Total Fat: 5g; Saturated Fat: 1g; Cholesterol: 83mg; Sodium: 417mg; Carbohydrates: 6g; Fiber: 1g; Protein: 26g*

# Charcuterie Board Bread

**SERVES 6**

*I didn't think there was a way to up the ante on a charcuterie board until we rolled all the components up into one loaf and served it warm. No need to worry about decorating or garnishing here, but feel free to serve this with different chutneys or sauces on the side for dipping. This is a fun and different way to serve everyone's favorite starter.* —by Kara Bleday

**NUT-FREE**

**Prep Time:** 10 minutes
**Total Cook Time:**
45 minutes
**Steam:** about 15 minutes
**Cook:** 30 minutes

**Accessories:** Ninja®
Multi-Purpose Pan or
8-inch round pan, Deluxe
Reversible Rack (bottom
layer only)

½ cup water, for steaming

Nonstick cooking spray

All-purpose flour,
  for dusting

1 (16-ounce) package
  store-bought pizza
  dough, at room
  temperature

2 ounces herbed finishing
  butter, melted

3 ounces salami,
  thinly sliced

2 ounces prosciutto,
  in large pieces

1½ cups shredded
  mozzarella
  cheese, divided

3 ounces pepperoni, sliced

1. Pour the water into the pot. Line the Multi-Purpose Pan with parchment paper and spray with cooking spray. Set aside.

2. Lightly flour a clean, flat work surface. Using a rolling pin dusted with flour, roll out the dough into a 28-by-48-inch rectangle. On one half of the dough, spread the herb butter in an even layer, then evenly cover with the salami, prosciutto, and 1 cup of mozzarella. Pull the other half of the dough up over the filling to make a square. There is no need to seal the edges.

3. Using a pizza cutter, cut the dough horizontally into 2-inch strips. Then, slice it vertically into 2-inch pieces. This will create equal squares of dough, meat, and mozzarella.

**4.** Take one square and roll it into a loose ball. Place the ball into the prepared pan. Repeat with the remaining dough squares.

**5.** Divide the pepperoni and the remaining ½ cup of mozzarella between the tops of the dough balls.

**6.** Place the pan on the bottom layer of the Deluxe Reversible Rack in the lower position, then place the rack in the pot.

**7.** Close the lid and move the slider to STEAMCRISP. Select STEAM & CRISP, set the temperature to 325°F, and set the time to 30 minutes. Press START/STOP to begin cooking (PrE will display for about 15 minutes as the unit steams, then the timer will start counting down). If the bread gets too brown during the cooking process, loosely cover it with aluminum foil and continue cooking.

**8.** When cooking is complete, the surface of the bread will be crusty and brown. Remove the rack and pan from the pot. Allow the bread to cool for 5 minutes before serving.

*Per serving: Calories: 469; Total Fat: 27g; Saturated Fat: 13g; Cholesterol: 77mg; Sodium: 1291mg; Carbohydrates: 36g; Fiber: 2g; Protein: 21g*

**Variation Tip:**
Try incorporating alternative cheeses, such as Gruyère or Havarti, to take your charcuterie bread to the next level.

# Giant Soft Pretzel with Beer Cheese

**SERVES 4**

*Pretzels and cheese sauce are a true match made in heaven. With the help of SteamCrisp™ technology, the pretzel achieves the most glorious golden brown and crispy exterior with a light and fluffy interior. Paired with the beer cheese, it will send your taste buds to space. This giant pretzel may be meant to be shared, but trust me when I say you could eat the whole thing yourself . . . it's just that good!* —by Caroline Schliep

**NUT-FREE**
**VEGETARIAN**

**Prep Time:** 10 minutes
**Total Cook Time:**
35 minutes
**Steam:** about 20 minutes
**Cook:** 10 minutes
**Sear/Sauté:** 5 minutes

**Accessories:** Deluxe Reversible Rack (bottom layer only)

1 (12-ounce) can lager beer

Nonstick cooking spray

1 cup plus 2 tablespoons self-rising flour

1 cup plain Greek yogurt

All-purpose flour, for dusting

¼ cup warm water

2 teaspoons baking soda

1 teaspoon garlic powder

1 teaspoon onion powder

Coarse salt

1 (16-ounce) block processed cheese product

2 cups grated pepper Jack cheese

1 cup grated sharp cheddar cheese

Kosher salt

Freshly ground black pepper

1. Pour the beer into the pot. Place the bottom layer of the Deluxe Reversible Rack in the higher position, then cover it with aluminum foil. Spray the foil with cooking spray. Place the rack in the pot.

2. To prepare the dough, combine the self-rising flour and yogurt in a large bowl and work until a smooth ball of dough forms.

3. Dust a clean, flat work surface with all-purpose flour. Place the dough on the surface and use your hands to form it into a 24-inch-long rope. Twist the rope into a pretzel shape.

*CONTINUED >*

**4.** In a shallow dish, whisk together the water and baking soda until dissolved. Dip both sides of the pretzel in the mixture, then place it on top of the foil in the pot. Sprinkle the pretzel with the garlic powder, onion powder, and some salt.

**5.** Close the lid and move the slider to STEAMCRISP. Select STEAM & CRISP, set the temperature to 340°F, and set the time to 10 minutes. Press START/STOP to begin cooking (PrE will display for about 20 minutes as the unit steams, then the timer will start counting down).

**6.** When cooking is complete, carefully remove the rack with the pretzel and set aside to cool. Leave the remaining beer in the pot.

**7.** To make the cheese sauce, move the slider to AIR FRY/ STOVETOP. Select SEAR/SAUTÉ and set the temperature to HI-5. Press START/STOP to begin cooking.

**8.** Add the processed cheese, pepper Jack, and cheddar to the pot with the beer. Season with salt and pepper and stir constantly until combined and melted, about 5 minutes.

**9.** Immediately pour the hot beer cheese into a bowl and serve with the pretzel.

**Substitution Tip:** If you can't find self-rising flour, you can substitute all-purpose flour mixed with 1½ teaspoons of baking powder.

*Per serving: Calories: 886; Total Fat: 55g; Saturated Fat: 32g; Cholesterol: 175mg; Sodium: 3160mg; Carbohydrates: 44g; Fiber: 1g; Protein: 47g*

# Dehydrated Fruit

**SERVES 1 TO 4**

*When I was younger, I worked at a juice bar that would dehydrate their own granola and it was amazing! I was so fascinated by dehydrating food. But the idea of buying this huge (and expensive) box of a machine that can only do one thing was silly. Now, years later, here I am working with a machine that can do it all! I am glad I held out on that dehydrator because now I can get even better results with the Ninja® Foodi® SmartLid™.* —by Athia Landry

DAIRY-FREE
GLUTEN-FREE
NUT-FREE
VEGAN

**Prep Time:** 5 minutes
**Total Cook Time:**
7 to 8 hours

**Accessories:** Deluxe
Reversible Rack
(both layers)

**Hack It:** You can dehydrate as little or as much fruit as you'd like with the same temperature and time. Alter this recipe to fit your needs!

1 to 3 cups hulled, halved strawberries (or cut into ½-inch pieces)

1 to 4 ripe bananas, peeled, cut into ⅜-inch pieces

1. Place the bottom layer of the Deluxe Reversible Rack in the lower position. Place the strawberries on the rack, then place the rack in the pot. It is okay if the berries touch, because they will decrease in size as they dehydrate.

2. Slide the Deluxe Layer through the lower layer's handles, then place the bananas on the Deluxe Layer. It is okay if they touch, because they will decrease in size as they dehydrate.

3. Close the lid and move the slider to AIR FRY/ STOVETOP. Select DEHYDRATE, set the temperature to 135ºF, and set the time to 7 hours. Press START/STOP to begin cooking.

4. After 7 hours, open the lid and check the doneness. If you like the fruit crispier, close the lid, select DEHYDRATE, set the temperature to 135ºF, and set the time to 1 hour. Press START/STOP to begin cooking.

5. When cooking is complete, remove the rack layers from the pot. Let the fruit cool before enjoying. Store the dehydrated fruit in an airtight container for up to 1 week.

*Per serving: Calories: 158; Total Fat: 1g; Saturated Fat: 0g; Cholesterol: 0mg; Sodium: 3mg; Carbohydrates: 40g; Fiber: 6g; Protein: 2g*

# Stuffed Mushrooms

**SERVES 4 TO 8**

*I despised mushrooms growing up. My sister used to love them, but I was just not a fan. I have no idea what changed, but one day I was at a family party and someone brought stuffed mushrooms with cheese and sausage, and they just looked and smelled so good. I decided to try them and fell in love. Now I throw mushrooms in as many things as possible, mainly stuffed or sautéed. If you aren't a fan of mushrooms, hopefully these will change your mind like they did mine.*
—by Melissa Celli

**NUT-FREE**

**Prep Time:** 10 minutes
**Total Cook Time:**
25 minutes
**Sear/Sauté:** 10 minutes
**Air Fry:** 15 minutes

**Accessories:** Cook & Crisp™ Basket

1 pound ground sausage

1 medium white onion, diced

1 teaspoon minced garlic

½ cup shredded Parmesan cheese

1 (5.2-ounce) block cow's milk garlic and herb cheese

2 tablespoons chopped fresh parsley, divided

¼ cup seasoned panko bread crumbs

Kosher salt

Freshly ground black pepper

10 to 12 large white mushrooms, cleaned, stems removed

1. Close the lid and move the slider to AIR FRY/STOVETOP. Select SEAR/SAUTÉ and set the temperature to HI-5. Open the lid and select START/STOP to begin preheating.

2. After 5 minutes, put the sausage in the pot and sauté for about 5 minutes, stirring frequently with a silicone spatula and breaking up the sausage into small pieces. Add the onion and garlic and sauté for another 5 minutes. Transfer the mixture to a large bowl. Scrape any bits off the bottom of the pot and wipe away any remaining oil.

**3.** To the sausage mixture, add the Parmesan, garlic and herb cheese, 1 tablespoon of parsley, and the bread crumbs. Season with salt and pepper and stir until evenly combined.

**4.** Stuff each mushroom with 1 to 2 tablespoons of the sausage mixture, allowing some to spill over the top.

**5.** Place the stuffed mushrooms in the Cook & Crisp™ Basket, then place the basket in the pot. Select AIR FRY, set the temperature to 350°F, and set the time to 15 minutes. Press START/STOP to begin cooking.

**6.** When cooking is complete, remove the mushrooms from the basket and top with the remaining 1 tablespoon of parsley. Serve immediately.

*Per serving: Calories: 607; Total Fat: 48g; Saturated Fat: 19g; Cholesterol: 122mg; Sodium: 1291mg; Carbohydrates: 13g; Fiber: 1g; Protein: 29g*

**Variation Tip:** For a vegetarian version, replace the sausage with a plant-based version or remove the sausage altogether and use 2 cups of finely chopped mushrooms, cooking them in place of the sausage in step 1.

# Fried Ravioli

**SERVES 4**

*If you're always looking for an interesting appetizer or snack, look no further. Everyone loves ravioli, and this recipe takes the typical deep-fried appetizer to a whole new, healthier level. What's also great about this recipe is that you can adjust it to your preference by using whatever ravioli filling you prefer, or you can use a mix. Another bonus is that you can use the sauce of your choice, whether that be marinara, a spicy chili sauce, or even ranch.* —by Jennie Vincent

**NUT-FREE**

**Prep Time:** 15 minutes
**Total Cook Time:** 8 to 24 minutes
**Cook:** 8 to 24 minutes

**Accessories:** Cook & Crisp™ Basket

Nonstick cooking spray

1 cup all-purpose flour

2 large eggs, beaten

1 cup panko bread crumbs

¼ cup grated Parmesan cheese, plus more for garnish

1 teaspoon dried basil

Kosher salt

Freshly ground black pepper

1 (9-ounce) package ravioli of choice, fresh or frozen (thawed if frozen)

1 cup warmed marinara or sauce of choice

1. Spray the Cook & Crisp™ Basket with cooking spray. Prepare the dredging station by placing the flour in a medium bowl, the eggs in a separate medium bowl, and in a third medium bowl mix together the bread crumbs, Parmesan, and basil. Season with salt and pepper.

2. Dredge each piece of pasta in the flour, shaking off any excess. Dip it in the eggs, and then in the bread crumb mixture, evenly coating both sides. Place the ravioli in the prepared basket in a single layer. Only prepare as many ravioli as will fit in the basket without touching or overlapping; you may need to work in batches.

*CONTINUED >*

**Fried Ravioli** continued

3. Place the basket in the pot. Close the lid and move the slider to AIR FRY/STOVETOP. Select AIR FRY, set the temperature to 390ºF, and set the time to 8 minutes. Press START/STOP to begin cooking.

4. When the first batch is complete, carefully remove the basket, place the toasted ravioli on a plate, and repeat steps 3 and 4 with the remaining ravioli, if necessary.

5. When cooking is complete, sprinkle the ravioli with Parmesan cheese and serve warm with the marinara dipping sauce.

**Per serving:** *Calories: 365; Total Fat: 10g; Saturated Fat: 4g; Cholesterol: 158mg; Sodium: 788mg; Carbohydrates: 49g; Fiber: 3g; Protein: 19g*

# General Tso's Cauliflower Bites

*This is a vegetable-based adaptation of one of the most popular takeout dishes, General Tso's Chicken. It's a great way to satisfy those deep-fried cravings without feeling weighed down, and these cauliflower bites are so good, you won't feel like you're missing out. I love to cook these for my best friend's kids when they stop by "Kelly's Restaurant" for dinner. Picky eaters won't bat an eyelash when their veggies are this tasty—I bet they won't even notice.* —by Kelly Gray

DAIRY-FREE
NUT-FREE
VEGETARIAN

**Prep Time:** 10 minutes
**Total Cook Time:**
30 minutes
**Preheat:** about 5 minutes
**Cook:** 25 minutes

**Accessories:** Cook & Crisp™ Basket

**Substitution Tip:** Substitute Buffalo sauce for the General Tso's sauce for a fiery kick!

2 large eggs, beaten

4 cups panko bread crumbs

1 head cauliflower, cut into 2-inch florets

1 cup prepared General Tso's sauce

2 scallions, chopped

1. Pour the beaten eggs into a medium bowl. Put the bread crumbs in a separate medium bowl.

2. Dredge the cauliflower florets in the egg, then evenly coat in the bread crumbs. Place the cauliflower in a single layer in the Cook & Crisp™ Basket.

3. Close the lid and move the slider to the AIR FRY/ STOVETOP position. Select AIR FRY, set the temperature to 400°F, and set the time to 25 minutes. Select START/ STOP to preheat the unit for 5 minutes.

4. After 5 minutes, place the basket in the pot and close the lid to begin cooking.

5. When cooking is complete, carefully remove the basket and transfer the cauliflower to a bowl. Pour the sauce over the cauliflower and toss until evenly coated. Garnish with the scallions and serve warm.

**Per serving:** *Calories: 388; Total Fat: 6g; Saturated Fat: 2g; Cholesterol: 93mg; Sodium: 1236mg; Carbohydrates: 68g; Fiber: 6g; Protein: 13g*

# Mac and Pimento Cheese Bites

SERVES 10 TO 12

*Pimento cheese is a snack staple in our household. Also known as Carolina caviar, this rich and pungent mixture of cheese and pimiento peppers, a true Southern classic, is sure to transform your macaroni and cheese. This recipe involves a little bit of prep, a little bit of waiting, but a lotta bit of flavor, so make sure you are organized and ready to go. These bites are perfect for those big holiday parties where you are really looking to wow your guests.* —by Craig White

**NUT-FREE**

**Prep Time:** 5 minutes, plus 4 hours to chill
**Total Cook Time:** 37 minutes
**Pressure Build:** about 15 minutes
**Pressure Cook:** 2 minutes
**Pressure Release:** 10 minutes
**Air fry:** 10 minutes

**Accessories:** 13-by-9-inch baking dish, Cook & Crisp™ basket

- 1 (12-ounce) can evaporated milk
- 4 cups water
- 1 (1-pound) box dry elbow pasta
- Kosher salt
- Freshly ground black pepper
- 2 tablespoons unsalted butter
- 2 cups prepared pimento cheese
- 1 cup Alfredo sauce
- 1 (8-ounce) bag shredded sharp cheddar cheese, divided
- Nonstick cooking spray
- 1 cup all-purpose flour
- 5 large eggs
- 3 cups garlic and herb bread crumbs

1. Combine the evaporated milk, water, and pasta in the pot. Season with salt and pepper and stir.

2. Close the lid and move the slider to PRESSURE. Make sure the pressure release valve is in the SEAL position. Select PRESSURE, set the temperature to LOW, and set the time to 2 minutes. Press START/STOP to begin cooking (the unit will build pressure for about 15 minutes before cooking begins).

3. When cooking is complete, select KEEP WARM and naturally release the pressure for 10 minutes, then quick release any remaining pressure by turning the pressure release valve to the VENT position. Once the pressure is released, move the slider to AIR FRY/STOVETOP to unlock the lid, then carefully open it.

**4.** Stir the macaroni, then add the butter, pimento cheese, Alfredo sauce, and cheddar cheese. Season with salt and pepper and stir to combine.

**5.** Spray a 13-by-9-inch baking dish with cooking spray. Pour the pasta into the prepared dish and cover the dish with plastic wrap, pushing the plastic down to press and compact the pasta. Refrigerate and let cool and set completely, 4 to 5 hours.

**6.** Once set, leaving the pasta in the dish, cut it into 64 equal pieces.

**7.** Prepare the dredging station by placing the flour in a medium bowl. Season with salt and pepper. Pour the eggs into a separate medium bowl. In a third medium bowl, season the bread crumbs with salt and pepper.

**8.** Carefully remove a mac and cheese bite from the dish and toss it in the flour, shaking to remove excess flour. Then dip it in the eggs, then in the bread crumbs, evenly coating all sides. Repeat with each bite.

**9.** Place 16 cheese bites in the Cook & Crisp™ Basket, then place the basket in the pot. Close the lid and move the slider to AIR FRY/STOVETOP. Select AIR FRY, set the temperature to 390ºF, and set the time to 10 minutes. Select START/STOP to begin cooking.

**10.** When cooking is complete, remove the bites from the basket. Repeat step 9 three more times with the remaining bites.

**Hack It:** This recipe makes 64 bites. Feel free to fry what you need and freeze the rest for future use. Prepare the bites through step 8, then lay them in a single layer in a resealable freezer bag and freeze for up to 1 month.

*Per serving: Calories: 617; Total Fat: 33g; Saturated Fat: 19g; Cholesterol: 148mg; Sodium: 673mg; Carbohydrates: 53g; Fiber: 2g; Protein: 27g*

# Korean-Sauced Chicken Wings

*I am a chicken wing connoisseur; I try them whenever they are on the menu. My fiancé and I love a restaurant near our home that serves the perfect wings; juicy on the inside and so crispy on the outside. I've never been able to replicate them— until now. With the Ninja® Foodi® SmartLid™ and SteamCrisp™ technology, I can elevate my wings to a whole new level.* —by Meg Jordan

DAIRY-FREE
GLUTEN-FREE
NUT-FREE

**Prep Time:** 5 minutes
**Total Cook Time:**
30 minutes
**Steam:** about 10 minutes
**Cook:** 20 minutes

**Accessories:** Cook & Crisp™ Basket

**Ingredient Info:** Make sure not to buy gochujang paste, which is different than gochujang sauce. Gochujang paste is a thick and spicy paste made from red chile pepper flakes, sticky rice, fermented soybeans, and salt. Gochujang sauce that you can buy in most supermarkets may include other ingredients in addition to the paste, such as honey, vinegar, and sesame oil.

½ cup water, for steaming

2 pounds frozen chicken wings

1 tablespoon canola oil

½ cup store-bought gochujang sauce

Kosher salt

Freshly ground black pepper

1. Pour the water into the pot.

2. In a medium bowl, toss the chicken wings with the oil until evenly coated.

3. Place the wings in the Cook & Crisp™ Basket and place the basket in the pot.

4. Close the lid and move the slider to STEAMCRISP. Select STEAM & CRISP, set the temperature to 400°F, and set the time to 20 minutes. Press START/STOP to begin cooking (PrE will display for about 10 minutes as the unit steams, then the timer will start counting down).

5. When cooking is complete, carefully remove the basket from the pot. Transfer the wings to a medium bowl with the gochujang sauce, season with salt and pepper, and toss to combine. Serve immediately.

**Per serving:** *Calories: 554; Total Fat: 36g; Saturated Fat: 9g; Cholesterol: 252mg; Sodium: 471mg; Carbohydrates: 16g; Fiber: 1g; Protein: 41g*

# Poutine

SERVES 4

*Poutine is a Canadian staple consisting of French fries, cheese curds, and a rich brown gravy. This stick-to-your ribs dish is the perfect comfort food for those long, dark winter nights we get so many of in New England. Steam-Crisped potatoes are deliciously fluffy on the inside and crispy on the outside, making them the perfect vessel for toppings. I like to finish my poutine with a heavy hand of cracked black pepper to add a little heat and cut some of the richness.* —by Kelly Gray

**GLUTEN-FREE**
**NUT-FREE**

**Prep Time:** 5 minutes, plus 30 minutes to soak
**Total Cook Time:** 43 minutes
**Steam:** about 8 minutes
**Cook:** 35 minutes

**Accessories:** Cook & Crisp™ Basket

- 1 gallon (16 cups) water, for soaking potatoes
- 3 tablespoons plus 1 teaspoon kosher salt, divided
- 3 tablespoons distilled white vinegar
- 1 pound russet potatoes, cut into ¼-inch sticks (peel on or peeled)
- 1 tablespoon canola oil
- 2 cups beef stock
- 1 cup cheese curds
- 1 (0.87-ounce) package dried brown gravy mix
- Freshly ground black pepper

1. In a large bowl, combine the water, 3 tablespoons of salt, the vinegar, and potatoes. Soak the potatoes for 30 minutes, then drain and pat dry with a clean kitchen towel.

2. In a medium bowl, toss the dried potatoes with the oil and remaining 1 teaspoon of salt. Place the potatoes in the Cook & Crisp™ Basket.

3. Pour the beef stock into the pot. Place the basket in the pot.

**4.** Close the lid and move the slider to STEAMCRISP. Select STEAM & CRISP, set the temperature to 450ºF, and set the time to 35 minutes. Select START/STOP to begin cooking (PrE will display for about 8 minutes as the unit steams, then the timer will start counting down).

**5.** When the time reads 17 minutes, open the lid and give the basket a shake to toss the potatoes. Close the lid and continue cooking. With 3 minutes remaining, open the lid and add the cheese curds. Close the lid to finish cooking.

**6.** When cooking is complete, remove the basket and transfer the potatoes to a serving plate.

**7.** Add the gravy packet to the stock in the pot. Using a silicone whisk, stir until the sauce has thickened.

**8.** Pour the gravy over the fries, top with black pepper, and serve warm.

---

*Per serving: Calories: 244; Total Fat: 12g; Saturated Fat: 5g; Cholesterol: 22mg; Sodium: 1082mg; Carbohydrates: 25g; Fiber: 2g; Protein: 10g*

**Substitution Tip:** Make it vegan: Substitute vegetable stock, vegan mozzarella, and a mushroom gravy packet.

Eggplant Parmesan, *page 78*

# 5

# Vegetarian Main Dishes

Eggplant Parmesan with Broccoli and Penne Marinara 78

Barbecue Cauliflower Tacos with Cabbage Slaw and Avocado 80

Whole Indian-Spiced Cauliflower with Curry Sauce 82

Vegetarian Chili with Cheesy Biscuits 84

Teriyaki Tofu with Ginger White Rice and Mushrooms 87

Miso-Garlic Risotto with Roasted Root Vegetables 90

Spicy Peanut Tofu Udon Bowls with Steamed Broccoli 92

Banh Mi Bowls with Crispy Tofu and Sriracha Mayonnaise 94

Twice-Baked Cheddar Broccoli Potatoes 97

Zucchini Boats Stuffed with Plant-Based Sausage 99

# Eggplant Parmesan with Broccoli and Penne Marinara

## SERVES 4 TO 6

*This recipe is filling, delicious, and comforting—but without any meat! People are clamoring for ethical and sustainable meal choices without losing out on flavor and satisfaction. This recipe is proof that you don't have to compromise; you still get a saucy pasta, crisp broccoli, and crunchy and cheesy eggplant.*

—by Sam Ferguson

**NUT-FREE**
**STEAMCRISP MEALS**

**Prep Time:** 20 minutes
**Total Cook Time:**
29 minutes
**Preheat:** about 14 minutes
**Steam & Crisp:** 10 minutes
**Broil:** 5 minutes

**Accessories:** Deluxe
Reversible Rack
(both layers)

½ cup all-purpose flour

Kosher salt

Freshly ground
black pepper

1 large egg

1 cup bread crumbs

½ cup grated
Parmesan cheese

1 medium (4- to 6-ounce)
eggplant, cut into
1-inch-thick rounds

**LEVEL 1 (BOTTOM OF POT)**
4½ cups (1½ [24-ounce)]
jars marinara sauce

2½ cups vegetable stock

1 (16-ounce) box dry
penne pasta

**LEVEL 2 (BOTTOM LAYER OF RACK)**
1 head broccoli (about
8 ounces), cut into
2-inch florets

**LEVEL 3 (TOP LAYER OF RACK)**
4 ounces mozzarella
cheese, cut in
½-inch slices

1. To prepare the dredging station, pour the flour into a medium bowl. Season with salt and pepper. Put the egg in a separate medium bowl and whisk. In a third medium bowl, mix the bread crumbs and Parmesan cheese.

2. Season one side of each eggplant round with salt and pepper. Dredge the seasoned side of each round in the flour, then dip in the egg, and place facedown in the bread crumb mixture. Set the eggplant rounds aside on a plate.

**3.** Place the marinara sauce and pasta in the pot and stir until combined.

**4.** Lay a 15-inch-long sheet of aluminum foil on a flat surface. Put the broccoli in the center and fold the edges of the foil in to create a sealed packet. Place the foil packet on the bottom layer of the Deluxe Reversible Rack in the lower position, then place the rack in the pot over the pasta mixture.

**5.** Slide the Deluxe Layer through the lower layer's handles. Place the eggplant rounds, breaded-side up, on the Deluxe Layer.

**6.** Close the lid and move the slider to STEAMCRISP. Select STEAM & CRISP, set the temperature to 390°F, and set the time to 10 minutes. Press START/STOP to begin cooking (PrE will display for about 14 minutes as the unit steams, then the timer will start counting down).

**7.** When cooking is complete, open the lid and place the mozzarella slices on top of the eggplant rounds.

**8.** Close the lid and move the slider to AIR FRY/STOVETOP. Select BROIL and set the time to 5 minutes. Press START/STOP to begin cooking.

**9.** When cooking is complete, carefully remove the entire rack with the eggplant and the foil packet.

**10.** Stir the pasta and serve with the broccoli and eggplant Parmesan.

**Substitution Tip:** To convert this recipe to chicken Parmesan, substitute 4 (4-ounce) chicken cutlets for the eggplant rounds in step 2. Adjust the cooking time to 12 minutes.

*Per serving: Calories: 785; Total Fat: 13g; Saturated Fat: 6g; Cholesterol: 74mg; Sodium: 898mg; Carbohydrates: 135g; Fiber: 15g; Protein: 34g*

# Barbecue Cauliflower Tacos with Cabbage Slaw and Avocado

**SERVES 2**

*Tacos are a great dinner option. I always have the ingredients for this recipe on hand, so it has become one of my favorites. Everything comes together so quickly, especially the cauliflower. The Ninja® Foodi® SmartLid™ steams and crisps the cauliflower to perfection. The best part is that you can set the unit and prepare the rest of the meal in the same amount of time and even make yourself a drink!*
—by Athia Landry

DAIRY-FREE
GLUTEN-FREE
NUT-FREE
VEGETARIAN

**Prep Time:** 15 minutes
**Total Cook Time:**
35 minutes
**Steam:** about 10 minutes
**Cook:** 25 minutes

**Accessories:** Cook & Crisp™ Basket

½ cup water, for steaming

1 head cauliflower, cut into 1-inch florets

¼ to ½ cup prepared barbecue sauce

Kosher salt

Freshly ground black pepper

2 cups shredded red cabbage

Juice of 1 lime

¼ cup mayonnaise

¼ cup chopped fresh cilantro

6 tortillas of choice

1 avocado, thinly sliced

1 jalapeño, thinly sliced

2 scallions, thinly sliced

1 lime, cut into wedges

1. Pour the water into the pot.

2. In a medium bowl, combine the cauliflower and barbecue sauce. Season with salt and pepper and toss until the cauliflower florets are evenly coated.

3. Place the cauliflower in the Cook & Crisp™ Basket and place the basket in the pot.

4. Close the lid and move the slider to STEAMCRISP. Select STEAM & CRISP, set the temperature to 425°F, and set the time to 25 minutes. Press START/STOP to begin cooking (PrE will display for about 10 minutes as the unit steams, then the timer will start counting down).

**5.** While the cauliflower is cooking, make the slaw. In a medium bowl, combine the shredded cabbage, lime juice, mayonnaise, and cilantro. Season with salt and pepper and toss until evenly combined. Set aside.

**6.** When cooking is complete, remove the cauliflower from the basket. Top the tortillas with cabbage slaw, cauliflower, avocado, jalapeño, and scallions. Serve with lime wedges.

**Per serving:** *Calories: 696; Total Fat: 39g; Saturated Fat: 6g; Cholesterol: 12mg; Sodium: 751mg; Carbohydrates: 84g; Fiber: 20g; Protein: 14g*

**Variation Tip:** If you prefer your tacos less spicy, replace the jalapeños with thinly sliced bell peppers.

# Whole Indian-Spiced Cauliflower with Curry Sauce

SERVES 4

*This recipe feels extra "cheffy" because of the whole cauliflower preparation and the South Asian–inspired seasoning flair, but it's simple to execute. When you score the surface of the cauliflower, you're not only promoting the development of flavor throughout the whole cauliflower head, you're also tenderizing the vegetable and making it easier to serve and enjoy at the dinner table. You shouldn't even need a knife once it is cooked—the pressure cooking will break down the cauliflower and allow you to serve and eat with only a fork!* —by Sam Ferguson

DAIRY-FREE
GLUTEN-FREE
NUT-FREE
VEGAN

**Prep Time:** 10 minutes
**Total Cook Time:**
21 minutes
**Pressure Build:** about
8 minutes
**Cook:** 3 minutes
**Pressure Release:** Quick
**Broil:** 10 minutes

**Accessories:** Cook & Crisp™ Basket

- 1 teaspoon ground coriander
- 1½ teaspoons ground cumin
- 1½ teaspoons garam masala
- 1 teaspoon turmeric
- 1 teaspoon mustard powder
- Kosher salt
- Freshly ground black pepper
- 1 (14- to 18-ounce) head cauliflower, whole with stem and leaves trimmed
- ¾ cup vegetable stock
- ½ cup prepared tikka masala curry sauce
- 1 tablespoon chopped fresh parsley

1. In a small bowl, combine the coriander, cumin, garam masala, turmeric, and mustard powder. Season with salt and pepper and mix thoroughly.

2. Using a sharp knife, score the cauliflower by making long, ¼-inch-deep cuts on the surface of the cauliflower. Using your hands, coat the surface of the cauliflower liberally with the prepared spice mix. Be sure to work the spice into the natural crevices and scores.

3. Pour the vegetable stock and curry sauce into the pot and stir to combine. Place the cauliflower head in the Cook & Crisp™ Basket. Place the basket in the pot.

**4.** Close the lid and move the slider to PRESSURE. Make sure the pressure release valve is in the SEAL position. Select PRESSURE. The temperature will default to HIGH. Use the arrows on the left to adjust the pressure setting to LOW. Use the arrows on the right to adjust the time to 3 minutes. Select START/STOP to begin cooking (the unit will build pressure for about 8 minutes before cooking begins).

**5.** When cooking is complete, select KEEP WARM and quick release the pressure by turning the pressure release valve to the VENT position. Once the pressure is released, move the slider to the AIR FRY/STOVETOP position. Select BROIL and set the time to 10 minutes. Press START/STOP to begin cooking.

**6.** When cooking is complete, open the lid and remove the basket from the pot. Stir the sauce. Place the cauliflower on a serving plate, then pour the sauce over the top. Garnish with the parsley and serve hot.

**Substitution Tip:** If you don't want to make your own spice rub for the cauliflower in step 1, you can use any generic ground curry spice from the spice aisle in your local grocery store.

**Per serving:** *Calories: 57; Total Fat: 1g; Saturated Fat: 0g; Cholesterol: 0mg; Sodium: 334mg; Carbohydrates: 11g; Fiber: 4g; Protein: 4g*

# Vegetarian Chili with Cheesy Biscuits

**SERVES 8**

*I love topping pressure-cooked meals with prepared foods such as mozzarella sticks, jalapeño poppers, and in this case, biscuit dough. Canned biscuit dough is versatile, forgiving, and delicious. The canned biscuits in this recipe should have a natural seam in the middle (to promote rising during baking) where you can peel them apart into two pieces each; this will help them cook all the way through when they're placed on top of the chili after pressure cooking. If you like, try swapping in a can of black beans and a can of chickpeas for two of the cans of kidney beans. —by Sam Ferguson*

**NUT-FREE**
**VEGETARIAN**

**Prep Time:** 20 minutes
**Total Cook Time:** 46 minutes
**Sear/Sauté:** 10 minutes
**Pressure Build:** about 14 minutes
**Cook:** 7 minutes
**Pressure Release:** Quick
**Bake:** 12 minutes
**Broil:** 3 minutes

1 tablespoon canola oil

1 small yellow onion, chopped

2 celery stalks, chopped

1 red bell pepper, seeded and chopped

1 yellow bell pepper, seeded and chopped

4 garlic cloves, minced

2 carrots, chopped

1 tablespoon ground cumin

1 tablespoon dried oregano

2 tablespoons chili powder

Kosher salt

Freshly ground black pepper

2 (4-ounce) cans chopped green chiles

2 (14-ounce) cans crushed tomatoes

3 (15-ounce) cans kidney beans, drained and rinsed

½ cup vegetable stock

1 cup frozen corn

4 uncooked canned biscuits, halved (for 2 biscuit rounds each)

1 cup shredded cheddar cheese

1. Close the lid and move the slider to AIR FRY/STOVETOP. Select SEAR/SAUTÉ and set the temperature to HI-5. Open the lid and select START/STOP and allow the unit to preheat for 5 minutes.

2. When the unit has preheated, pour the oil into the pot. Add the onion, celery, red bell pepper, yellow bell pepper, garlic, carrots, cumin, oregano, and chili powder. Season with salt and pepper. Sauté until the vegetables are tender, about 10 minutes.

CONTINUED >

**Substitution Tip:** This is a great "kitchen sink" recipe. You can replace any of the canned beans with other varieties or swap any of the fresh vegetables for other options in your refrigerator (such as mushrooms or kale).

**Variation Tip:** Make this recipe vegan by skipping the prepared biscuits and using your favorite vegan cheddar cheese, or omitting cheese altogether.

3. Add the green chiles, tomatoes, kidney beans, and vegetable stock and stir to combine.

4. Close the lid and move the slider to PRESSURE. Make sure the pressure release valve is in the SEAL position. Select PRESSURE. The temperature will default to HIGH, which is the correct setting. Use the arrows on the right to adjust the time to 7 minutes. Select START/STOP to begin cooking (the unit will build pressure for about 14 minutes before cooking begins).

5. When cooking is complete, select KEEP WARM and quick release the pressure by turning the pressure release valve to the VENT position. Once the pressure is released, move the slider to the AIR FRY/STOVE TOP position, then carefully open the lid. Add the corn to the pot and stir. Place the biscuit dough pieces on top of the chili.

6. Close the lid. Select BAKE, set the temperature to 300°F, and set the time to 12 minutes. Select START/STOP to begin cooking.

7. When cooking is complete, open the lid and sprinkle the cheddar cheese over the biscuits.

8. Close the lid, select BROIL, and set the time to 3 minutes. Select START/STOP to begin cooking.

9. When cooking is complete, serve warm.

**Per serving:** *Calories: 348; Total Fat: 10g; Saturated Fat: 3g; Cholesterol: 15mg; Sodium: 537mg; Carbohydrates: 52g; Fiber: 11g; Protein: 17g*

# Teriyaki Tofu with Ginger White Rice and Mushrooms

**SERVES 4**

*The template for this recipe is a favorite in my house—flavorful rice, steamed vegetables, and crispy glazed tofu. Cooking this recipe traditionally is easy enough, but it requires lots of pots and pans, and you have to use both the stovetop and the oven. When dinner is over, I'm always the sucker who must do the dishes. With the Ninja® Foodi® SmartLid™, there's only half as much to clean and it's all dishwasher safe! Cooking this recipe in the SmartLid™ has given me that dishwashing time back—more time to relax and decompress after a long day.*

—by Sam Ferguson

DAIRY-FREE
GLUTEN-FREE
NUT-FREE
STEAMCRISP MEALS
VEGAN

**Prep Time:** 15 minutes, plus 1 hour to marinate
**Total Cook Time:** 19 minutes
**Steam:** about 9 minutes
**Steam & Crisp:** 10 minutes

**Accessories:** Deluxe Reversible Rack (both layers)

**LEVEL 1 (BOTTOM OF POT)**
1 tablespoon minced fresh ginger

2 garlic cloves, minced

½ cup shredded carrots

1 cup long-grain white rice, rinsed

2 cups water

Kosher salt

Freshly ground black pepper

**LEVEL 2 (BOTTOM LAYER OF RACK)**
1 (8-ounce) package button mushrooms, halved

**LEVEL 3 (TOP LAYER OF RACK)**
1 (16-ounce) package extra-firm tofu, drained, patted dry, and cut into 1-inch cubes

1 cup prepared gluten-free teriyaki marinade

4 scallions, cut into 1-inch pieces

1. Start with the Level 3 ingredients: Combine the tofu and teriyaki marinade in a resealable plastic bag. Place the tofu in the refrigerator for at least 1 hour and up to 8 hours.

2. Once the tofu is marinated, place the ginger, garlic, carrots, rice, and water in the pot, season with salt and pepper, and stir to combine.

*CONTINUED >*

## Teriyaki Tofu with Ginger White Rice and Mushrooms continued

**Ingredient Info:** This recipe is vegan and gluten-free, provided you source the correct teriyaki sauce—depending on the brand, some will contain gluten and may not be vegan. If this is a priority for you, be sure to read the label.

**3.** Place the bottom level of the Deluxe Reversible Rack in the lower position, then place the rack in the pot. Place the mushrooms on top of the rack.

**4.** Slide the Deluxe Layer through the lower layer's handles, then cover with aluminum foil. Place the marinated tofu and scallions on the Deluxe Layer.

**5.** Close the lid and move the slider to STEAMCRISP. Select STEAM & CRISP, set the temperature to 450°F, and set the time to 10 minutes. Press START/STOP to begin cooking (PrE will display for about 9 minutes as the unit steams, then the timer will start counting down).

**6.** When cooking is complete, carefully remove the entire rack with the tofu and the mushrooms. Stir the rice and serve with the tofu and mushrooms.

**Per serving:** *Calories: 362; Total Fat: 7g; Saturated Fat: 1g; Cholesterol: 0mg; Sodium: 1,345mg; Carbohydrates: 55g; Fiber: 3g; Protein: 21g*

# Miso-Garlic Risotto with Roasted Root Vegetables

*I love risotto, including the act of making it on the stove. There is something really relaxing about slowly adding the liquid and constantly stirring to get the perfect consistency. Sadly, making risotto is a time-consuming process and therefore I don't make it that often. But that has changed with the Ninja® Foodi® SmartLid™. I can now make risotto in less than 30 minutes, and it requires far less stirring. This recipe calls for miso, which is not a typical risotto ingredient, but it adds a delicious umami flavor that pairs perfectly with the butter and scallions. Each bite is a perfect blend of Asian and Italian flavors.* —by Athia Landry

GLUTEN-FREE
NUT-FREE
STEAMCRISP MEALS
VEGETARIAN

**Prep Time:** 15 minutes
**Total Cook Time:**
28 minutes
**Sear/Sauté:** 3 minutes
**Steam:** 15 minutes
**Cook:** 10 minutes

**Accessories:** Deluxe Reversible Rack (bottom layer only)

## LEVEL 1 (BOTTOM OF POT)

3 tablespoons unsalted butter

2 scallions, thinly sliced, white and green parts separated, divided

3 garlic cloves, thinly sliced

1 tablespoon white miso paste

1 cup arborio rice

3 cups vegetable broth

## LEVEL 2 (BOTTOM LAYER OF RACK)

1 tablespoon sesame oil

1 carrot, diced

1 red or golden beet, uncooked, peeled and diced

Kosher salt

Freshly ground black pepper

**1.** Close the lid and move the slider to AIR FRY/STOVETOP. Select SEAR/SAUTÉ and set the temperature to 4. Open the lid and select START/STOP to begin preheating. Allow the unit to preheat for 5 minutes.

**2.** Start with the Level 1 ingredients: When the unit has preheated, put the butter, white parts of the scallions, garlic, and miso paste into the pot. Cook, stirring often, until fragrant, about 3 minutes.

**3.** Select START/STOP to stop the cooking process. Add the rice and broth and stir until combined.

**4.** Put the sesame oil, carrot, and beet in a large bowl, season with salt and pepper, and toss until fully combined. Lay a 15-inch-long sheet of aluminum foil on a flat surface. Pour the Level 2 vegetable mixture onto the center and fold the edges of the foil in to create a sealed packet. Place the foil packet on the bottom layer of the Deluxe Reversible Rack in the lower position, then place the rack in the pot over the rice mixture.

**5.** Close the lid and move the slider to STEAMCRISP. Select STEAM & CRISP, set the temperature to 450°F, and set the time to 10 minutes. Press START/STOP to begin cooking (PrE will display for about 15 minutes as the unit steams, then the timer will start counting down).

**6.** When cooking is complete, carefully remove the rack with the foil packet. Stir the risotto, serve with the root vegetables, and top with the green parts of the scallions.

*Per serving: Calories: 647; Total Fat: 25g; Saturated Fat: 12g; Cholesterol: 46mg; Sodium: 1,043mg; Carbohydrates: 95g; Fiber: 6g; Protein: 9g*

**Variation Tip:** The addition of miso paste in the risotto allows you to omit the salt. Make sure you taste the risotto before serving and season with salt, if necessary.

# Spicy Peanut Tofu Udon Bowls with Steamed Broccoli

**SERVES 2**

*I'll be honest: Tofu isn't my first option for a protein substitution. However, when it's cooked in a delicious sauce, my mind can be changed easily. I love this spicy peanut sauce because of its versatility. The peanut butter can be switched out for any nut butter, or even sunflower butter if you have a nut allergy. And if spice isn't your thing, simply omit it or add lime juice to balance out the spiciness.*
—by Athia Landry

DAIRY-FREE
STEAMCRISP MEALS
VEGAN

**Prep Time:** 20 minutes
**Total Cook Time:**
21 minutes
**Steam:** about 8 minutes
**Cook:** 13 minutes

**Accessories:** Deluxe
Reversible Rack
(both layers)

**LEVEL 1 (BOTTOM OF POT)**
½ cup water, for steaming

**LEVEL 2 (BOTTOM LAYER OF RACK)**

2 heaping cups
broccoli florets

4 scallions, thinly sliced,
green and white parts
separated, divided

1 tablespoon sesame oil

Kosher salt

Freshly ground
black pepper

**LEVEL 3 (TOP LAYER OF RACK)**

2 tablespoons water

1 tablespoon soy sauce

2 tablespoons creamy
peanut butter

1 tablespoon chili
garlic sauce, plus
more for serving

¼ cup sesame oil

2 garlic cloves, minced

2 tablespoons minced
fresh ginger

1 (14.5-ounce) package
extra-firm tofu, drained,
patted dry, and cut
into 1-inch pieces

4 ounces udon
noodles, cooked

Sesame seeds, for serving

1. Pour the water into the pot.

2. Combine the broccoli, white parts of the scallions, and sesame oil in a medium bowl, season with salt and pepper, and toss well. Lay a 15-inch-long sheet of aluminum foil on a flat surface. Put the broccoli onto the center and fold the edges of the foil in to create a sealed packet. Place the foil packet on the bottom layer of the Deluxe Reversible Rack in the lower position, then place the rack in the pot.

3. Cover the Deluxe Layer with another sheet of foil, then slide the Deluxe Layer through the lower layer's handles.

4. Prepare the Level 3 ingredients: Whisk together the water, soy sauce, peanut butter, chili garlic sauce, sesame oil, garlic, and ginger in a large bowl. Add the tofu one piece at a time to the sauce, toss to evenly coat all sides, then place on the Deluxe Layer. Repeat with the remaining tofu. It is okay if the tofu pieces touch each other on the rack.

5. Close the lid and move the slider to STEAMCRISP. Select STEAM & CRISP, set the temperature to 390°F, and set the time to 13 minutes. Press START/STOP to begin cooking (PrE will display for about 8 minutes as the unit steams, then the timer will start counting down).

6. When cooking is complete, divide the cooked udon between two bowls. Top with spicy peanut tofu, steamed broccoli, the green parts of the scallions, and sesame seeds. Top with any remaining sauce and additional chili garlic sauce, if desired.

**Per serving:** *Calories: 837; Total Fat: 55g; Saturated Fat: 8g; Cholesterol: 0mg; Sodium: 936mg; Carbohydrates: 62g; Fiber: 6g; Protein: 36g*

# Banh Mi Bowls with Crispy Tofu and Sriracha Mayonnaise

**SERVES 2**

*Traditionally, a banh mi is a delicious Vietnamese sandwich made with pâté, ham, pickled vegetables, and cilantro. Other versions are made with sliced pork, pork belly, or sausage. As a vegetarian, I miss out on this delicious sandwich. Fear not, though—this banh mi bowl has all the familiar flavors of the sandwich, but with a veg-friendly twist. Each bite has the perfect combination of sweet, sour, and spicy.*
—by Athia Landry

DAIRY-FREE
GLUTEN-FREE
NUT-FREE
STEAMCRISP MEALS
VEGAN

**Prep Time:** 15 minutes
**Total Cook Time:** 30 minutes
**Steam:** about 15 minutes
**Cook:** 15 minutes

**Accessories:** Deluxe Reversible Rack (bottom layer only)

**LEVEL 1 (BOTTOM OF POT)**

2 cups sushi rice

3 cups water

1 tablespoon minced fresh ginger

Kosher salt

**LEVEL 2 (TOP LAYER OF RACK)**

2 tablespoons cornstarch

1 teaspoon garlic powder

Kosher salt

Freshly ground black pepper

1 (14.5-ounce) package extra-firm tofu, drained, patted dry, and cut into 1-inch pieces

Nonstick cooking spray

Sweet chili sauce

2 tablespoons sriracha

¼ cup mayonnaise

Juice of 1 lime

Kosher salt

Pickled vegetables (carrots, cucumber, radish), as desired

¼ cup chopped fresh cilantro

2 scallions, thinly sliced

1. Combine the rice, water, ginger, and salt in the pot and stir.

2. In a large bowl, combine the cornstarch and garlic powder. Season with salt and pepper. Add the tofu and carefully toss until the tofu is evenly coated.

**3.** Place the Deluxe Reversible Rack in the lower position and cover with a sheet of aluminum foil greased with cooking spray, then place the rack in the pot. Place the tofu on the foil. Brush the top of the tofu with the sweet chili sauce. as desired.

**4.** Close the lid and move the slider to STEAMCRISP. Select STEAM & CRISP, set the temperature to 390°F, and set the time to 15 minutes. Press START/STOP to begin cooking (PrE will display for about 15 minutes as the unit steams, then the timer will start counting down).

**5.** While the rice and tofu cook, prepare the sauce. In a small bowl, whisk together the sriracha, mayonnaise, lime juice, and some salt.

**6.** When cooking is complete, remove the rack with the tofu from the pot. Stir the rice and serve with the tofu, pickled vegetables, cilantro, scallions, and sriracha mayonnaise.

*Per serving: Calories: 1,113; Total Fat: 33g; Saturated Fat: 5g; Cholesterol: 12mg; Sodium: 570mg; Carbohydrates: 169g; Fiber: 7g; Protein: 34g*

**Substitution Tip:** Want to pickle your own vegetables? Combine 1 cup of water, 1 cup of white vinegar, 1 tablespoon of kosher salt, and 1 tablespoon of granulated sugar in a small saucepan and bring to a boil. Stir until the salt and sugar have dissolved, then remove the pan from the heat. Pour the pickling liquid over your vegetables. Allow the vegetables to pickle in an airtight container in the refrigerator for at least 48 hours before eating.

**Variation Tip:** If you don't like spice, switch out the sriracha for sweet chili sauce (not spicy, despite the name) or grate garlic into the mayonnaise for a garlic aioli. All options are equally delicious.

# Twice-Baked Cheddar Broccoli Potatoes

| SERVES 4 |

*The Ninja® Foodi® SmartLid™ has taken my love for potatoes to the next level. I am always willing to spend a little extra time cooking to put potatoes on my plate, but now I don't have to wait! The SmartLid™ steams and crisps whole potatoes in 35 minutes. Yes, I know, how amazing! You know what else is amazing? This recipe is sneakily vegan.* —by Athia Landry

**GLUTEN-FREE**
**NUT-FREE**
**VEGAN**

**Prep Time:** 15 minutes
**Total Cook Time:**
48 minutes
**Steam:** 8 minutes
**Cook:** 35 minutes
**Broil:** 5 minutes

**Accessories:** Deluxe Reversible Rack (bottom layer only)

1 cup water, for steaming

4 medium russet potatoes, poked several times with a fork

1 heaping cup coarsely chopped broccoli florets

1 cup vegan cheddar cheese, divided

¾ cup vegan sour cream

4 pieces cooked plant-based bacon, chopped

1 teaspoon garlic powder

Kosher salt

Freshly ground black pepper

1. Pour the water into the pot. Place the bottom layer of the Deluxe Reversible Rack in the lower position in the pot. Place the potatoes on the rack.

2. Close the lid and move the slider to STEAMCRISP. Select STEAM & CRISP, set the temperature to 400ºF, and set the time to 35 minutes. Press START/STOP to begin cooking (PrE will display for about 8 minutes as the unit steams, then the timer will start counting down).

3. When cooking is complete, remove the potatoes and allow them to cool for about 5 minutes. Make a 2-inch cut along the length of each potato. Scoop out the flesh and transfer it to a large bowl, leaving the potato skins intact.

*CONTINUED >*

**4.** Add the broccoli, ½ cup of cheddar cheese, the sour cream, plant-based bacon, and garlic powder to the bowl. Season with salt and pepper and mash until fully mixed with the potatoes.

**5.** Stuff the potato mixture back inside the potato skins, then sprinkle the stuffed skins with the remaining ½ cup of cheddar cheese. Place the stuffed potatoes on the rack in the pot.

**6.** Close the lid and move the slider to AIR FRY/ STOVETOP. Select BROIL and set the time to 5 minutes. Press START/STOP to begin broiling.

**7.** When cooking is complete, remove the twice-baked potatoes and serve warm.

*Per serving: Calories: 575; Total Fat: 21g; Saturated Fat: 13g; Cholesterol: 20mg; Sodium: 878mg; Carbohydrates: 79g; Fiber: 6g; Protein: 21g*

# Zucchini Boats Stuffed with Plant-Based Sausage

**SERVES 2**

*These zucchini boats make a great first course for a dinner party or an appealing option for kids. Any way you look at it, they'll be a crowd favorite because they taste amazing and are completely vegetarian! Don't miss the tip at the bottom of the recipe; the sausage stuffing for the zucchini boats can easily be converted into a tasty and versatile meatball mix.* —by Sam Ferguson

**NUT-FREE**

**Prep Time:** 15 minutes
**Total Cook Time:**
22 minutes
**Steam:** about 7 minutes
**Cook:** 15 minutes

**Accessories:** Deluxe Reversible Rack (bottom layer only)

**Variation Tip:** This recipe also makes a great plant-based meatball—simply combine all the ingredients (except the zucchini boats) and use as a substitute for your favorite meatball-based recipe.

- 2 (6-inch) zucchini, halved lengthwise
- 2 links spicy plant-based sausage, crumbled
- 1 small yellow onion, chopped
- 3 garlic cloves, minced
- 1 tomato, chopped (about ½ cup)
- Kosher salt
- Freshly ground black pepper
- ¼ cup grated Parmesan cheese
- ¼ cup bread crumbs
- 2 tablespoons extra-virgin olive oil
- ¼ cup shredded mozzarella cheese
- ½ cup water, for steaming
- Nonstick cooking spray
- 2 tablespoons chopped fresh parsley

1. Using a spoon, scoop the flesh out of each zucchini half and put it in a medium bowl. Remove as much as you can while leaving the outer peel intact (it's your boat).

2. Add the sausage, onion, garlic, and tomato to the bowl with the zucchini flesh. Season with salt and pepper and mix well.

3. In a separate medium bowl, combine the Parmesan cheese, bread crumbs, and olive oil and mix well.

4. Stuff the sausage mixture evenly into the zucchini boats. Cover each zucchini boat with half the Parmesan mixture, then with half the mozzarella cheese.

*CONTINUED >*

**5.** Pour the water into the pot. Place the bottom layer of the Deluxe Reversible Rack in the lower position and spray it with cooking spray. Place the zucchini boats on the rack, then place the rack in the pot.

**6.** Close the lid and move the slider to STEAMCRISP. Select STEAM & CRISP, set the temperature to 375ºF, and set the time to 15 minutes. Press START/STOP to begin cooking (PrE will display for about 7 minutes as the unit steams, then the time will start counting down).

**7.** When cooking is complete, open the lid and remove the zucchini boats from the rack. Garnish with the parsley and serve hot.

**Per serving:** *Calories: 372; Total Fat: 26g; Saturated Fat: 7g; Cholesterol: 22mg; Sodium: 686mg; Carbohydrates: 23g; Fiber: 5g; Protein: 16g*

**Almond-Crusted Salmon, Broccoli, and Quinoa with Leeks,** *page 104*

# 6

# Seafood Main Dishes

# Almond-Crusted Salmon, Broccoli, and Quinoa with Leeks

**SERVES 4**

*The Ninja® Foodi® SmartLid™ and its new SteamCrisp™ technology are perfect for cooking complete meals, even when using delicate proteins such as salmon. For this recipe, layered quinoa, broccoli, and almond-crusted salmon make a quick and easy weeknight meal all in one pot. Simply prep the meal components, assemble, set the unit, and press start—you'll have a well-balanced meal in 30 minutes.* —by Kelly Gray

**GLUTEN-FREE STEAMCRISP MEALS**

**Prep Time:** 10 minutes
**Total Cook Time:**
27 minutes
**Sear/Sauté:** 5 minutes
**Steam:** about 15 minutes
**Cook:** 7 minutes

**Accessories:** Deluxe Reversible Rack (both layers)

**LEVEL 1 (BOTTOM OF POT)**

2 tablespoons salted butter

1 leek, white and light green parts, thinly sliced

3 cups vegetable stock

2 cups white quinoa, rinsed

**LEVEL 2 (BOTTOM LAYER OF RACK)**

1 head broccoli, cut into 2-inch florets

Kosher salt

Freshly ground black pepper

**LEVEL 3 (TOP LAYER OF RACK)**

1 cup sliced almonds, finely chopped

Grated zest of 1 lemon

1 tablespoon chopped fresh parsley

2 tablespoons canola oil

Kosher salt

Freshly ground black pepper

2 large eggs

4 (6-ounce) salmon fillets

1. Close the lid and move the slider to AIR FRY/STOVETOP. Select SEAR/SAUTÉ and set the temperature to 3. Open the lid and select START/STOP to begin preheating. Allow the unit to preheat for 5 minutes.

2. Once the unit has preheated, put the butter in the pot and stir until melted. Add the leek and stir until evenly coated in butter. Cook for 5 minutes, stirring occasionally, until golden brown and fragrant. Press START/STOP to stop cooking.

**3.** Add the stock and quinoa to the pot and stir until combined with the leek.

**4.** Lay a 15-inch-long sheet of aluminum foil on a flat surface. Put the broccoli in the center, season with salt and pepper, and fold the edges of the foil in to create a sealed packet.

**5.** Place the foil packet on the bottom layer of the Deluxe Reversible Rack in the lower position, then place the rack in the pot over the quinoa mixture. Slide the Deluxe Layer through the lower layer's handles.

**6.** Prepare the almond topping for the salmon by combining the almonds, lemon zest, parsley, and oil in a medium bowl. Season with salt and pepper. Crack the **eggs** into a shallow bowl and whisk them.

**7.** Dip one side of each salmon fillet (if using skin-on fillets, dip the flesh side) in the egg and then dredge in the almond mixture. Place each fillet on top of the Deluxe Layer in the pot, crumb-side up.

**8.** Close the lid and move the slider to STEAMCRISP. Select STEAM & CRISP, set the temperature to 425°F, and set the time to 7 minutes. Press START/STOP to begin cooking (PrE will display for about 15 minutes as the unit steams, then the timer will start counting down).

**9.** When cooking is complete, carefully remove the rack layer with the salmon, then the rack layer with the broccoli.

**10.** Stir the quinoa and serve warm with the salmon and broccoli.

**Per serving:** *Calories: 904; Total Fat: 43g; Saturated Fat: 8g; Cholesterol: 202mg; Sodium: 293mg; Carbohydrates: 74g; Fiber: 13g; Protein: 58g*

# Frozen Teriyaki Salmon, Green Beans, and Rice Pilaf

**SERVES 4**

*I admit it—my freezer can get so packed that I often forget what I have in there. Sometimes weeknight meals turn into a game of "what's in the freezer?" With other appliances, it's really difficult to get a great texture on frozen protein if I forget to thaw it out first. Not anymore! With the Ninja® Foodi® SmartLid™, I can create meals any time of the week with those treasures I find in my freezer.*
—by Meg Jordan

NUT-FREE
STEAMCRISP MEALS

**Prep Time:** 10 minutes plus 8 hours to marinate
**Total Cook Time:** 25 minutes
**Steam:** about 15 minutes
**Cook:** 10 minutes

**Accessories:** Deluxe Reversible Rack (both layers)

**LEVEL 1 (BOTTOM OF POT)**
**2 (6-ounce) boxes rice pilaf, plus ingredients called for in box instructions**

**LEVEL 2 (MIDDLE LAYER OF RACK)**
**1 (12-ounce) bag trimmed green beans**

**2 tablespoons canola oil, divided**

**Kosher salt**

**Freshly ground black pepper**

**LEVEL 3 (TOP LAYER OF RACK)**
**4 (6-ounce) fresh, skinless salmon fillets**

**1 (16-ounce) bottle teriyaki marinade**

1. Start with the Level 3 ingredients: Place the salmon and teriyaki marinade in a large resealable freezer bag. Seal the bag and move the salmon around to coat it thoroughly with marinade. Transfer the salmon to a baking sheet, then place it in the freezer for at least 8 hours and up to 24 hours.

2. Once the salmon is frozen and marinated, place the rice and ingredients called for in the box instructions in the pot and stir until combined.

3. Place the bottom layer of the Deluxe Reversible Rack in the lower position, then place the rack in the pot over the rice mixture.

**4.** Prepare the Level 2 ingredients: In a large bowl, toss the green beans with the oil, and season with salt and pepper. Lay a 15-inch-long sheet of aluminum foil on a flat surface. Put the green beans in the center and fold the edges of the foil in to create a sealed packet. Place the foil packet on the bottom layer of the rack.

**5.** Remove the salmon fillets from the marinade and place them on the top layer of the rack.

**6.** Close the lid and move the slider to STEAMCRISP. Select STEAM & CRISP, set the temperature to 400°F, and set the time to 10 minutes. Press START/STOP to begin cooking (PrE will display for about 15 minutes as the unit steams, then the timer will start counting down).

**7.** When cooking is complete, carefully remove the rack layers with the salmon and green beans.

**8.** Stir the rice and serve with the salmon and green beans.

*Per serving: Calories: 777; Total Fat: 18g; Saturated Fat: 3g; Cholesterol: 77mg; Sodium: 1923mg; Carbohydrates: 94g; Fiber: 3g; Protein: 56g*

# Cajun Fish and Andouille Sausage Dirty Rice

**SERVES 2 TO 3**

*I love Cajun food, but I have never really thought of its heritage. In researching it, I found out that a lot of Cajun people came from Nova Scotia, just like my family. This could be the reason I am so partial to the cuisine, but I think it's the spice. Cajun food tends to have a kick, and this recipe is no different. If spicy food isn't your thing, feel free to season with a spice blend of your choice.* —by Craig White

GLUTEN-FREE
NUT-FREE
STEAMCRISP MEALS

**Prep Time:** 10 minutes
**Total Cook Time:**
31 minutes
**Sear/Sauté:** 6 minutes
**Steam:** about 20 minutes
**Cook:** 5 minutes

**Accessories:** Deluxe Reversible Rack (bottom layer only)

1 tablespoon canola oil

2 fully cooked andouille sausages, diced

1 bell pepper, seeded and diced

1 celery stalk, diced

½ small white onion, diced

1 garlic clove, minced

2 tablespoons unsalted butter

1 tablespoon plus 1 teaspoon Cajun spice rub, divided

3 (6-ounce) fresh tilapia fillets

2 cups white rice

4 cups beef stock

1. Close the lid and move the slider to AIR FRY/STOVETOP. Select SEAR/SAUTÉ and set the temperature to HI-5. Open the lid and select START/STOP to begin preheating. Allow the unit to preheat for 5 minutes.

2. When the unit has preheated, put the oil, sausage, bell pepper, celery, and onion in the pot and sauté, stirring often, until the onion is tender, 5 to 6 minutes.

3. Add the garlic, butter, and 1 teaspoon of Cajun spice rub to the pot, and cook for 30 seconds, stirring constantly with a rubber spatula to incorporate.

4. While the vegetables and sausage are cooking, rub both sides of the tilapia fillets with the remaining 1 tablespoon of Cajun spice rub.

*CONTINUED >*

**Variation Tip:** Not a fan of tilapia? Swap it out for a fresh piece of flounder.

**5.** Add the rice and beef stock to the pot and stir to combine.

**6.** Place the bottom layer of the Deluxe Reversible Rack in the higher position, then place the rack in the pot over the rice mixture. Place the fillets on the rack.

**7.** Close the lid and move the slider to STEAMCRISP. Select STEAM & CRISP, set the temperature to 450°F, and set the time to 5 minutes. Press START/STOP to begin cooking (PrE will display for about 20 minutes as the unit steams, then the timer will start counting down).

**8.** When cooking is complete, carefully remove the rack with the fish. Stir the rice and serve with the fish.

**Per serving:** *Calories: 1,435; Total Fat: 47g; Saturated Fat: 17g; Cholesterol: 205mg; Sodium: 948mg; Carbohydrates: 167g; Fiber: 7g; Protein: 81g*

# Homemade Fish Sticks and Broccoli

**SERVES 4**

*These homemade fish sticks are super quick and simple to make and will make you forget all about the ones from the freezer section in your grocery store. With the help of SteamCrisp™ technology, these fish sticks come out super-duper crunchy and golden brown on the outside, yet light and flaky on the inside. Trust me when I say your kids will keep coming back for more, even faster than you can make them.* —by Caroline Schliep

**DAIRY-FREE**
**NUT-FREE**
**STEAMCRISP MEALS**

**Prep Time:** 10 minutes
**Total Cook Time:**
35 minutes
**Steam:** about 20 minutes
**Cook:** 15 minutes

**Accessories:** Deluxe Reversible Rack (both layers)

**Substitution Tip:** Feel free to substitute halibut, haddock, catfish, or even tilapia for the cod. If using catfish or tilapia, which are much thinner fillets, reduce the cooking time to 5 minutes.

**LEVEL 1 (BOTTOM OF POT)**
½ cup water, for steaming

**LEVEL 2 (BOTTOM LAYER OF RACK)**
1 (12-ounce) head broccoli, cut into large florets

Kosher salt

Freshly ground black pepper

**LEVEL 3 (TOP LAYER OF RACK)**
Nonstick cooking spray

1 cup all-purpose flour

2 large eggs

2 cups panko bread crumbs

2 teaspoons garlic powder

2 teaspoons onion powder

1 teaspoon paprika

Kosher salt

Freshly ground black pepper

3 (6-ounce) frozen cod fillets, cut into ½-inch wide sticks

1. Pour the water into the pot. Place the bottom layer of the Deluxe Reversible Rack in the lower position, then place it in the pot.

2. In a medium bowl, season the broccoli with salt and pepper. Transfer the broccoli to the rack in the pot.

3. Prepare the Level 3 ingredients: Cover the top layer of the Deluxe Reversible Rack with a sheet of aluminum foil, then slide it through the lower layer's handles and spray with cooking spray.

CONTINUED >

**4.** Prepare a dredging station by placing the flour in a medium bowl. Crack the eggs into a separate medium bowl and whisk. In a third medium bowl, combine the bread crumbs, garlic powder, onion powder, and paprika. Season with salt and pepper and mix.

**5.** Dredge the fish sticks in the flour, shaking off any excess flour. Dip each fish stick in the eggs, then in the bread crumb mixture, evenly coating all sides. Place the fish sticks on the foil on the rack.

**6.** Close the lid and move the slider to STEAMCRISP. Select STEAM & CRISP, set the temperature to 390°F, and set the time to 15 minutes. Press START/STOP to begin cooking (PrE will display for about 20 minutes as the unit steams, then the timer will start counting down).

**7.** After 7 minutes, open the lid and flip the fish sticks. Close the lid to continue cooking.

**8.** When cooking is complete, carefully remove the entire rack. Serve the fish sticks with the steamed broccoli.

*Per serving: Calories: 310; Total Fat: 4g; Saturated Fat: 1g; Cholesterol: 106mg; Sodium: 710mg; Carbohydrates: 40g; Fiber: 4g; Protein: 29g*

# Fish and Chips

*I don't know about you, but because I don't love frying, I only have fish and chips occasionally. With the SteamCrisp one-touch meal system, you can not only have dinner on the table in around 40 minutes, but also a far heathier version. After all, by air frying, you barely use any oil at all.* —by Jennie Vincent

**DAIRY-FREE**
**NUT-FREE**
**STEAMCRISP MEALS**

**Prep Time:** 10 minutes, plus 30 minutes for soaking
**Total Cook Time:** 39 minutes
**Steam:** about 15 minutes
**Cook:** 24 minutes

**Accessories:** Cook & Crisp™ Basket

- **1 gallon (16 cups) water, for soaking, plus 1 cup water for steaming**
- **3 tablespoons kosher salt, plus more for seasoning**
- **1½ pounds russet potatoes, cut into ¼-inch wedges**
- **¼ cup all-purpose flour**
- **1 large egg**
- **½ cup panko bread crumbs**
- **Freshly ground black pepper**
- **2 (6-ounce) fresh haddock fillets**
- **2 tablespoons canola oil**
- **Lemon wedges, to serve**

1. Combine the gallon of water, 3 tablespoons of salt, and the potatoes in a large bowl. Soak for 30 minutes, then drain and pat the potatoes dry with a clean kitchen towel.

2. Prepare the dredging station by pouring the flour into a medium bowl. Crack the egg into a separate medium bowl and whisk it. Pour the bread crumbs into a third medium bowl, and season with salt and pepper.

3. Dredge one haddock fillet in the flour, shaking off any excess flour. Dip it in the egg, then in the bread crumb mixture, evenly coating both sides. Place on a plate. Repeat with the remaining fillet.

**4.** Pour the remaining 1 cup of water into the pot. In a large bowl, toss the potato wedges with the oil and season with salt and pepper. Transfer the wedges to the Cook & Crisp™ Basket and place the basket in the pot.

**5.** Close the lid and move the slider to STEAMCRISP. Select STEAM & CRISP, set the temperature to 450ºF, and set the time to 24 minutes. Press START/STOP to begin cooking (PrE will display for about 15 minutes as the unit steams, then the timer will start counting down).

**6.** After 12 minutes, open the lid and use tongs to carefully toss the fries. Place both haddock fillets on top of the fries. Close the lid and continue cooking.

**7.** When cooking is complete, carefully remove the basket. Serve the haddock with lemon wedges and fries.

**Per serving:** *Calories: 664; Total Fat: 18g; Saturated Fat: 2g; Cholesterol: 185mg; Sodium: 998mg; Carbohydrates: 83g; Fiber: 6g; Protein: 42g*

# Frozen Cod with Roasted Carrots and Curried Couscous

**SERVES 4**

*This meal is quick, easy, healthy, and delicious. Moroccan couscous has smaller grains than Israeli couscous, which are slightly thicker. The flavors of the couscous, carrots, and cod balance each other out very nicely—and preparing dinner is easy when you can cook them all together in the SmartLid™.* —by Myles Bryan

---

**DAIRY-FREE
NUT-FREE
STEAMCRISP MEALS**

---

**Prep Time:** 5 minutes
**Total Cook Time:**
22 minutes
**Steam:** about 15 minutes
**Cook:** 7 minutes

---

**Accessories:** Deluxe
Reversible Rack
(both layers)

**LEVEL 1 (BOTTOM OF POT)**

| | |
|---|---|
| **1 cup Moroccan couscous** | **Kosher salt** |
| **1½ cups water** | **Freshly ground** |
| **1 tablespoon curry powder** | **black pepper** |

**LEVEL 2 (BOTTOM LAYER OF RACK)**

**1 (12-ounce) bag
    frozen carrots**

**LEVEL 3 (TOP LAYER OF RACK)**

| | |
|---|---|
| **4 (6-ounce) frozen
    cod fillets** | **1 teaspoon onion powder** |
| | **Kosher salt** |
| **1 teaspoon canola oil** | **Freshly ground** |
| **1 teaspoon smoked paprika** | **black pepper** |

1. Put the couscous, water, and curry powder into the pot and season with salt and pepper in the pot and stir until combined.

2. Place the Deluxe Reversible Rack in the lower position and cover with a sheet of aluminum foil, then place the rack in the pot. Place the carrots on top of the foil.

3. Prepare the Level 3 ingredients: Evenly coat the cod fillets on both sides with the oil, paprika, and onion powder. Season with salt and pepper.

**4.** Slide the Deluxe Layer through the lower layer's handles. Place the cod fillets on the top layer of the rack.

**5.** Close the lid and move the slider to STEAMCRISP. Select STEAM & CRISP, set the temperature to 450°F, and set the time to 7 minutes. Press START/STOP to begin cooking (PrE will display for about 15 minutes as the unit steams, then the timer will start counting down).

**6.** When cooking is complete, carefully remove the rack layer with the cod, then the rack layer with the carrots. Stir the couscous and serve warm with the cod and roasted carrots.

**Per serving:** *Calories: 329; Total Fat: 3g; Saturated Fat: 0g; Cholesterol: 80mg; Sodium: 657mg; Carbohydrates: 42g; Fiber: 6g; Protein: 33g*

**Variation Tip:** For an even more filling meal, serve with naan bread.

# Mediterranean Halibut en Papillote-ish

**SERVES 4**

*Though cooking "en papillote" can sound intimidating, if you've ever made a foil pouch, then you're already there. This French technique is perfect for preparing fish or vegetables and helps create a tender, flavorful final dish. Traditionally the protein is wrapped in parchment paper, as I do in this recipe, but I've found that aluminum foil works just fine in a pinch, though it isn't as easily transferable to the table for a dramatic reveal.* —by Kara Bleday

**DAIRY-FREE**
**GLUTEN-FREE**
**NUT-FREE**

**Prep Time:** 5 minutes
**Total Cook Time:** 20 minutes

**Accessories:** Deluxe Reversible Rack (both layers)

1 cup water, for steaming

4 (5-ounce) fresh halibut fillets

1 cup cherry tomatoes, halved

1 tablespoon capers

4 tablespoons extra-virgin olive oil

½ cup kalamata olives, pitted and sliced

¾ cup roasted red pepper strips

2 tablespoons white wine

4 fresh basil leaves

Kosher salt

Freshly ground black pepper

1 large egg, beaten

1 lemon, cut into wedges, for serving

1. Pour the water into the pot.

2. Lay two large sheets of parchment paper on a flat surface. On each sheet, place 2 halibut fillets. Divide the tomatoes, capers, olive oil, olives, red peppers, wine, and basil leaves between the two sheets. Season with salt and pepper. Brush the edges of the parchment paper with the beaten egg. Fold the sides of the paper up and over the fish, sealing it into a neat packet.

**3.** Place the bottom layer of the Deluxe Reversible Rack in the lower position, then place it in the pot. Place one fish packet on the rack. Slide the Deluxe Layer through the lower layer's handles. Place the second fish packet on the Deluxe Layer.

**4.** Close the lid and move the slider to AIR FRY/ STOVETOP. Select STEAM and set the time to 20 minutes. Press START/STOP to begin cooking.

**5.** When cooking is complete, carefully remove both racks. To serve, gently tear the tops of the packets and release the steam. Scoop the fish and vegetables onto plates and serve with fresh lemon wedges.

**Substitution Tip:** For an easier seal, try using aluminum foil to make a neat pouch. No need for the beaten egg in that case.

*Per serving: Calories: 300; Total Fat: 18g; Saturated Fat: 3g; Cholesterol: 116mg; Sodium: 330mg; Carbohydrates: 4g; Fiber: 1g; Protein: 29g*

# Vietnamese-Inspired Shrimp and Noodle Soup

*This soup is inspired by pho, considered by many to be Vietnam's national dish. This staple soup traditionally simmers away for hours, creating a flavorful broth that is accompanied by rice noodles, herbs, and varying types of meat or poultry. Although this cooking method is unrivaled, making this soup by pressure cooking comes remarkably close to producing the same flavor but in nearly no time at all. This version puts yet another spin on the classic by adding shrimp. The thin rice noodles and tender shrimp pair beautifully in this flavorful broth.* —by Avery Lowe

DAIRY-FREE
NUT-FREE

**Prep Time:** 10 minutes
**Total Cook Time:**
25 minutes
**Pressure Build:** about
8 minutes
**Sear/Sauté:** 12 minutes
**Cook:** 5 minutes
**Pressure Release:** Quick

- 2 tablespoons sesame oil
- 3 tablespoons minced fresh ginger
- 5 large bok choy leaves, thinly sliced, stems discarded
- 2 teaspoons Chinese five-spice powder
- 8 cups chicken broth
- 1½ tablespoons soy sauce
- 1 tablespoon fish sauce
- 8 ounces thin rice noodles
- 1 pound (21–25 count) shrimp, fresh or thawed, peeled, deveined, with tails on

1. Close the lid and move the slider to AIR FRY/STOVETOP. Select SEAR/SAUTÉ and set the temperature to HI-5. Open the lid and select START/STOP to begin preheating. Allow the unit to preheat for 5 minutes. Put the oil, ginger, bok choy, and five-spice powder in the pot and sauté for 5 minutes. Add the broth, soy sauce, and fish sauce.

2. Close the lid. Press START/STOP to reset the unit. Move the slider to PRESSURE, making sure the pressure release valve is in the SEAL position. Select PRESSURE. The temperature will default to HIGH, which is the correct setting. Set the time to 5 minutes and press START/STOP to begin cooking (the unit will build pressure for about 8 minutes before cooking begins).

**3.** When cooking is complete, select KEEP WARM and quick release the pressure by turning the pressure release valve to the VENT position. Once the pressure is released, move the slider to AIR FRY/STOVETOP to unlock the lid, then carefully open it.

**4.** Add the noodles and shrimp to the pot, making sure they are submerged in the broth. Select SEAR/SAUTÉ and set the time to 7 minutes. Select START/STOP to begin cooking. Cook until the noodles are tender and the shrimp is pink and cooked through.

**5.** When cooking is complete, serve immediately.

**Per serving:** *Calories: 255; Total Fat: 5g; Saturated Fat: 1g; Cholesterol: 122mg; Sodium: 621mg; Carbohydrates: 33g; Fiber: 1g; Protein: 18g*

**Substitution Tip:** Can't find 21 to 25 count shrimp? You can substitute any large or extra-large peeled and deveined shrimp.

# Spicy Shrimp with Vegetables and Cilantro Rice

SERVES 4

*Bright colors, fresh flavors, and fragrant spices come together in this simple dish, perfect for a weeknight meal or margarita night. Marinated shrimp, vegetables, and cilantro rice are great on their own, but they also make the perfect starting point for shrimp tacos and burrito bowls—no need for extra dishes or steps.*

—by Kelly Gray

DAIRY-FREE
GLUTEN-FREE
NUT-FREE
STEAMCRISP MEALS

**Prep Time:** 10 minutes, plus 30 minutes to marinate
**Total Cook Time:** 40 minutes
**Steam:** about 15 minutes
**Cook:** 25 minutes

**Accessories:** Deluxe Reversible Rack (both layers)

**LEVEL 1 (BOTTOM OF POT)**

1 cup basmati rice, rinsed

1¾ cups water

Juice of 1 lime (about ¼ cup)

2 tablespoons chopped fresh cilantro

**LEVEL 2 (BOTTOM LAYER OF RACK)**

3 ears fresh corn, cut into 2-inch pieces

1 red onion, quartered

**LEVEL 3 (TOP LAYER OF RACK)**

2 teaspoons chili powder

1 teaspoon ground cumin

1 teaspoon kosher salt

1 tablespoon canola oil

Juice of 2 limes (about ½ cup)

2 tablespoons agave nectar

1 tablespoon chopped fresh cilantro

12 ounces fresh shrimp, peeled and deveined

6 baby bell peppers, whole

1. Start with the Level 3 ingredients: In a large bowl, whisk together the chili powder, cumin, salt, oil, lime juice, agave nectar, and cilantro until combined. Then place the marinade and shrimp in a large resealable plastic bag. Massage the outside of the bag to work the marinade over all parts of the shrimp. Place the bag in the refrigerator for 30 minutes to marinate.

2. After the shrimp are marinated, place the rice, water, lime juice, and cilantro in the pot and stir until combined.

*CONTINUED >*

**Substitution Tip:**
Replace the shrimp with boneless, skinless chicken thighs, and increase the cook time to 12 minutes.

**3.** Place the bottom layer of the Deluxe Reversible Rack in the lower position, cover it with a sheet of aluminum foil, then place it in the pot. Place the corn and onion (Level 2 ingredients) on top of the foil.

**4.** Slide the Deluxe Layer through the lower layer's handles. Remove the shrimp from the bag, discarding the marinade, and place the shrimp on the Deluxe layer with the baby bell peppers.

**5.** Close the lid and move the slider to STEAMCRISP. Select STEAM & CRISP, set the temperature to 375°F, and set the time to 25 minutes. Press START/STOP to begin cooking (PrE will display for about 15 minutes as the unit steams, then the timer will start counting down).

**6.** When cooking is complete, carefully remove the rack layer with the shrimp and peppers, then the rack layer with the corn and onion. Stir the rice and serve warm with the shrimp, peppers, onions, and corn.

**Per serving:** *Calories: 447; Total Fat: 6g; Saturated Fat: 1g; Cholesterol: 137mg; Sodium: 453mg; Carbohydrates: 78g; Fiber: 6g; Protein: 25g*

# Jambalaya

*Nothing beats a one-pot meal—starch, veggies, and protein, all cooked to perfection in the SmartLid™! This jambalaya makes enough to feed a crowd and is an impressive dish to serve your family and friends. Your guests will also be impressed by how calm, cool, and collected you will be when throwing a dinner party, because this meal couldn't be any easier.* —by Michelle Boland

**DAIRY-FREE**
**NUT-FREE**
**STEAMCRISP MEALS**

**Prep Time:** 5 minutes
**Total Cook Time:**
30 minutes
**Steam:** about 15 minutes
**Cook:** 15 minutes

**Substitution Tip:** Feel free to switch out the proteins. Don't like sausage? Use chicken. No seafood? Swap for pork tenderloin! If using chicken or pork, cut it into 1-inch cubes. Vegan plant-based meats work well, too.

2 (8-ounce) boxes jambalaya rice mix, plus ingredients called for in box instructions

1 cup frozen sliced okra

½ cup frozen sliced peppers and onions

12 ounces andouille sausage, thinly sliced

1 pound frozen uncooked shrimp, peeled with tail on

3 scallions, thinly sliced, for garnish

1. Put the jambalaya rice mix and ingredients called for in the box instructions, okra, peppers and onions, sausage, and shrimp in the pot and stir until evenly combined.

2. Close the lid and move the slider to STEAMCRISP. Select STEAM & CRISP, set the temperature to 350°F, and set the time to 15 minutes. Press START/STOP to begin cooking (PrE will display for about 15 minutes as the unit steams, then the timer will start counting down).

3. When cooking is complete, stir the jambalaya and allow it to sit for 5 minutes to absorb any remaining liquid. Serve warm, garnished with the scallions.

*Per serving: Calories: 550; Total Fat: 19g; Saturated Fat: 7g; Cholesterol: 165mg; Sodium: 1,129mg; Carbohydrates: 62g; Fiber: 3g; Protein: 32g*

# Seafood Stew

**SERVES 4 TO 6**

*Pressure cooking seems to be one of those cooking techniques that is slightly scary. I remember seeing pressure cookers on the stovetop on TV as a child and they seemed terrifying. The Ninja® Foodi® SmartLid™ really makes pressure cooking simple and easy. This recipe is a play on a classic chowder. It's more of a brothy-style chowder, but it's filled with great seafood and shellfish with some veggies and potatoes thrown in and finished with parsley for brightness. By pressure cooking for just a short time, the potatoes cook through and the seafood flavor really shines.* —by Melissa Celli

DAIRY-FREE
GLUTEN-FREE
NUT-FREE

**Prep Time:** 10 minutes
**Total Cook Time:**
45 minutes
**Pressure Build:** about
15 minutes
**Pressure Cook:** 5 minutes
**Pressure Release:** 5 to
10 minutes
**Sear/Sauté:** 15 minutes

1 tablespoon canola oil

4 celery stalks, chopped

1 medium white
   onion, chopped

2 teaspoons minced garlic

2 russet potatoes, chopped

1 (32-ounce) box
   seafood stock

1 (28-ounce) can
   diced tomatoes

1 cup (15 to 20) frozen
   cooked medium shrimp,
   peeled and tails removed

2 (16-ounce) bags frozen
   mixed seafood (e.g.,
   scallops, mussels,
   shrimp, squid)

2 teaspoons dried thyme

Kosher salt

Freshly ground
   black pepper

Chopped fresh parsley,
   for garnish

**1.** Close the lid and move the slider to AIR FRY/STOVETOP. Select SEAR/SAUTÉ and set the temperature to HI-5. Select START/STOP to begin preheating. Allow the unit to preheat for 5 minutes.

**2.** When the unit has preheated, pour in the oil. When the oil is hot, add the celery and onion to the pot and sauté, stirring frequently, for 5 minutes. Add the garlic and sauté for 1 minute. Add the potatoes and seafood stock.

**3.** Close the lid and move the slider to PRESSURE. Make sure the pressure release valve is in the SEAL position. Select PRESSURE. The temperature will default to HIGH, which is the correct setting. Set the time to 5 minutes. Press START/STOP to begin cooking (the unit will build pressure for about 15 minutes before cooking begins).

**4.** When cooking is complete, select KEEP WARM and quick release the pressure by turning the pressure release valve to the VENT position. Once all the pressure has released and the unit has indicated it is safe to open, open the lid. Move the slider to AIR FRY/STOVETOP. Select SEAR/SAUTÉ and set the temperature to HI-5. Press START/STOP to begin cooking.

**5.** Add the tomatoes, frozen shrimp, frozen seafood mixture, and thyme to the pot. Season with salt and pepper and stir to combine. Bring the mixture to a boil and cook until the seafood is cooked through, about 10 minutes.

**6.** When cooking is complete, serve the stew in bowls, topped with parsley.

**Per serving:** *Calories: 429; Total Fat: 6g; Saturated Fat: 1g; Cholesterol: 146mg; Sodium: 1034mg; Carbohydrates: 51g; Fiber: 7g; Protein: 45g*

**Substitution Tip:** If you cannot find frozen mixed seafood, feel free to use fresh shellfish such as clams, mussels, scallops, squid, shrimp, or any other variety you prefer. Add the fresh seafood in place of the frozen in step 5 after the stew has already come up to a boil, and cook the seafood for 3 to 4 minutes, until cooked through.

**Lemon and Honey Steam-Crisped Whole Chicken,** *page 130*

# 7

# Poultry Mains

# Lemon and Honey Steam-Crisped Whole Chicken

**SERVES 4**

*Whole roasted chicken is one of those foods that epitomizes warmth, coziness, and nourishment. The familiar and comforting smells of a roasting chicken will fill your kitchen and quickly bring people to the dinner table. When I was a kid, my great-aunt Gigi would make a whole roasted chicken on Sundays in the fall; on those days it was never a challenge to get the entire family around the dinner table. When you want to bring your own family together, try this recipe.*

—by Sam Ferguson

DAIRY-FREE
GLUTEN-FREE
NUT-FREE

**Prep Time:** 10 minutes
**Total Cook Time:** 1 hour 8 minutes
**Steam:** about 8 minutes
**Cook:** 1 hour

**Accessories:** Cook & Crisp™ Basket

1 (6-pound) whole chicken, giblets and neck removed, rinsed and patted dry

1 lemon, quartered, divided

4 rosemary sprigs, divided

1 head garlic, halved lengthwise

Kosher salt

Freshly ground black pepper

½ cup water, for steaming

2 tablespoons extra-virgin olive oil

1 teaspoon honey

1. Stuff the chicken cavity with 2 lemon quarters, 2 rosemary sprigs, and the halved garlic head. Season the surface of the chicken with salt and pepper.

2. Pour the water into the pot. Place the Cook & Crisp™ Basket in the pot, then place the chicken in the basket.

3. Close the lid and move the slider to STEAMCRISP. Select STEAM & CRISP, set the temperature to 360°F, and set the time to 60 minutes. Press START/STOP to begin cooking (PrE will display for about 8 minutes as the unit steams, then the time will star counting down).

**4.** While the chicken is cooking, prepare the honey glaze. Remove the leaves from the remaining 2 rosemary sprigs (discard the stems) and coarsely chop. In a small bowl, combine the rosemary, olive oil, and honey. Season with salt and pepper and stir to combine.

**5.** When there are 10 minutes remaining on the count-down timer, open the lid and baste the chicken liberally with the glaze. Close the lid to continue cooking.

**6.** When cooking is complete, open the lid and remove the basket from the pot. Remove the chicken from the basket and allow it to rest for at least 10 minutes before carving and serving.

*Per serving: Calories: 662; Total Fat: 48g; Saturated Fat: 13g; Cholesterol: 207mg; Sodium: 233mg; Carbohydrates: 2g; Fiber: 0g; Protein: 51g*

**Substitution Tip:** If you don't want to use rosemary, fresh thyme, sage, and parsley are great substitutions. The idea is to get as much flavor into and onto the chicken—use whatever fresh herbs you'd like.

# Chicken Cordon Bleu

**SERVES 3**

*Chicken cordon bleu is a traditional dish from Switzerland usually made with veal or chicken breast. This dish is the definition of comfort food: melty Swiss cheese and salty ham rolled up in a thinly pounded chicken breast, then fried. The beauty of using the Ninja® Foodi® SmartLid™ for this dish is that you air fry it, so you get all the crispiness of deep-frying without all the fat. This dish is always a crowd-pleaser and will leave your family satisfied. It is best served with some vegetables.*
—by Myles Bryan

**NUT-FREE**

**Prep Time:** 15 minutes
**Total Cook Time:**
29 minutes
**Steam:** about 15 minutes
**Cook:** 14 minutes

**Accessories:** Cook & Crisp™ Basket

¼ **cup water, for steaming**

3 **(5- to 6-ounce) boneless, skinless chicken breasts**

**Kosher salt**

**Freshly ground black pepper**

2 **tablespoons Dijon mustard**

6 **slices Swiss cheese**

6 **slices deli ham**

½ **cup all-purpose flour**

2 **large eggs**

2 **cups panko bread crumbs**

½ **cup grated Parmesan cheese**

1. Pour the water into the pot.

2. Place 1 chicken breast on a cutting board and with a sharp knife, butterfly the chicken by cutting the breast three-quarters of the way through horizontally (as if slicing a bagel). Open the breast up and cover with plastic wrap. Lightly pound the chicken with a mallet or rolling pin until it is ¼ inch thick. Repeat with the remaining chicken breasts.

3. Season each chicken breast with salt and pepper, then evenly cover in Dijon mustard on the open, cut side of the chicken. Place 2 slices of cheese and 2 slices of ham on each breast. Roll each breast up and secure with 2 toothpicks on each side.

4. Prepare the dredging station by pouring the flour into a medium bowl. Crack the eggs into a separate medium bowl and whisk. In a third medium bowl, combine the bread crumbs and Parmesan.

5. Dredge the outside of each chicken breast in the flour, shaking off any excess flour. Dip them in the eggs, then in the bread crumb mixture, evenly coating all sides. Place the chicken in the Cook & Crisp™ basket and place the basket in the pot.

6. Close the lid and move the slider to STEAMCRISP. Select STEAM & CRISP, set the temperature to 400°F, and set the time to 14 minutes. Press START/STOP to begin cooking (PrE will display for about 15 minutes as the unit steams, then the timer will start counting down).

7. When cooking is complete, remove the basket from the pot. Remove the toothpicks from the chicken and serve immediately.

*Per serving:* *Calories: 798; Total Fat: 39g; Saturated Fat: 17g; Cholesterol: 248mg; Sodium: 923mg; Carbohydrates: 39g; Fiber: 2g; Protein: 69g*

# Chicken Marsala with Roasted Red Potatoes

SERVES 4

*I have a fond childhood memory of chicken marsala. My nana would take the family out to dinner to a place called Augustine's on Route 1 in Saugus, Massachusetts. That was my first buffet experience, and I just couldn't wrap my head around the fact that I could keep eating . . . and that I did. I ate so much chicken marsala I could barely move. This recipe feeds four, but I guarantee your family will want more, so you might want to make another batch for second (or third) helpings.*

—by Craig White

**NUT-FREE**
**STEAMCRISP MEALS**

**Prep Time:** 10 minutes
**Total Cook Time:**
47 minutes
**Sear/Sauté:** 17 minutes
**Steam:** about 20 minutes
**Cook:** 10 minutes

**Accessories:** Deluxe Reversible Rack (both layers)

**LEVEL 1 (BOTTOM OF POT)**
½ **small white onion, diced**
3 **cups cremini mushrooms, sliced**
3 **cups chicken stock**
1 **cup marsala wine**
3 **tablespoons water**
3 **tablespoons cornstarch**
1 **tablespoon unsalted butter**

**LEVEL 2 (BOTTOM LAYER OF RACK)**
1 **pound baby red potatoes, halved**
1 **tablespoon canola oil**
**Kosher salt**
**Freshly ground black pepper**

**LEVEL 3 (TOP LAYER OF RACK)**
4 **(6-ounce) boneless, skinless chicken breasts**
**Kosher salt**
**Freshly ground black pepper**
¼ **cup all-purpose flour**
3 **tablespoons unsalted butter**

1. Close the lid and move the slider to AIR FRY/STOVETOP. Select SEAR/SAUTÉ and set the temperature to HI-5. Select START/STOP to preheat the unit.

*CONTINUED >*

**2.** While the unit is preheating, start with the Level 3 ingredients: Season the chicken on all sides with salt and pepper. Pour the flour into a shallow bowl. Coat the chicken in the flour, shaking to remove any excess flour.

**3.** When the unit has preheated, put the butter in the pot. Once the butter has melted, add the chicken breasts and sauté until browned, 3 to 4 minutes per side.

**4.** While the chicken cooks, prepare the Level 2 ingredients: In a large bowl, combine the potatoes and oil. Season with salt and pepper and toss until the potatoes are evenly coated.

**5.** When the chicken is done cooking, remove it from the pot and set aside. Prepare the Level 1 ingredients: Put the onion and mushrooms in the pot and cook for 5 minutes. Add the chicken stock and wine, scraping up any browned bits from the bottom of the pot.

**6.** Place the bottom layer of the Deluxe Reversible Rack in the lower position, cover with a sheet of aluminum foil, then place the rack in the pot over the mushroom mixture. Place the potatoes on the foil.

**7.** Slide the Deluxe Layer through the lower layer's handles. Place the chicken breasts on the Deluxe Layer.

**8.** Close the lid and move the slider to STEAMCRISP. Select STEAM & CRISP, set the temperature to 390ºF, and set the time to 10 minutes. Press START/STOP to begin cooking (PrE will display for about 20 minutes as the unit steams, then the timer will start counting down).

**9.** While the meal is cooking, in a small bowl, whisk together the water and cornstarch until combined and completely smooth.

**10.** When cooking is complete, carefully remove the entire rack with the chicken and potatoes. Select SEAR/SAUTÉ and set the temperature to HI-5. Select START/STOP and stir the cornstarch mixture into the sauce. Simmer for 3 to 4 minutes or until thickened. Stir in the butter (Level 1 ingredient) and season with salt and pepper.

**11.** Serve the chicken with the potatoes and mushroom sauce.

**Variation Tip:** Add 1 to 2 tablespoons of heavy (whipping) cream and a squeeze of fresh lemon juice to really take this marsala sauce to the next level.

*Per serving: Calories: 577; Total Fat: 20g; Saturated Fat: 8g; Cholesterol: 139mg; Sodium: 185mg; Carbohydrates: 40g; Fiber: 3g; Protein: 41g*

# Chicken Piccata with Polenta Cakes

**SERVES 6**

*The Ninja® Foodi® SmartLid™ and its SteamCrisp™ technology really makes this chicken piccata come to life. Here, chicken breasts, seared to a golden brown, with crispy polenta cakes are made on the Deluxe Reversible Rack. The contents in the bottom of the pot not only serve as the steaming liquid but also become a luscious lemony sauce. Searing the chicken ahead of time means the chicken takes less time to cook. In fact, by using the SteamCrisp function, everything can be cooked together and finished together for a true one-pot meal.* —by Melissa Celli

**NUT-FREE**
**STEAMCRISP MEALS**

**Prep Time:** 10 minutes
**Total Cook Time:**
40 minutes
**Sear/Sauté:** 15 minutes
**Steam:** about 15 minutes
**Cook:** 10 minutes

**Accessories:** Deluxe Reversible Rack (both layers)

**Substitution Tip:** If you feel that the sauce isn't thick enough, add a cornstarch slurry to the sauce in step 9. Whisk together 1 tablespoon each of cornstarch and water and pour into the sauce, whisking to incorporate. Simmer the sauce for several minutes to thicken.

### LEVEL 1 (BOTTOM OF POT)

- 1 teaspoon minced garlic
- 1 (3-ounce) jar capers, drained
- ½ cup white wine
- 1 cup chicken stock
- Juice of 1 lemon
- ¼ cup grated Parmesan cheese
- ½ cup heavy (whipping) cream
- Kosher salt
- Freshly ground black pepper
- Chopped parsley, for garnish

### LEVEL 2 (BOTTOM LAYER OF RACK)

- ½ cup all-purpose flour
- Kosher salt
- Freshly ground black pepper
- 6 (5- to 6-ounce) boneless, skinless chicken breasts
- 1 tablespoon canola oil

### LEVEL 3 (TOP LAYER OF RACK)

- 1 (18-ounce) tube prepared polenta, cut into 8 to 10 slices
- 3 tablespoons unsalted butter, cold, cut into cubes

1. Start with the Level 2 ingredients: Pour the flour into a large bowl, season with salt and pepper, and stir. Dredge each chicken breast in the flour and set aside.

2. Close the lid and move the slider to AIR FRY/STOVETOP. Select SEAR/SAUTÉ and set the temperature to HI-5. Select START/STOP to preheat the unit for 5 minutes.

**3.** When the unit is preheated, pour the oil into the pot. When the oil is hot, add the chicken to the pot and sear for about 6 minutes per side. Once seared, remove from the pot, leaving any browned bits in the bottom, and set aside.

**4.** Prepare the Level 1 ingredients: Add the garlic and capers to the pot and sauté for 30 seconds. Add the wine and gently scrape up any bits stuck to the bottom of the pot. Bring the mixture to a low boil, then add the chicken stock, lemon juice, and Parmesan and stir to combine.

**5.** Place the bottom layer of the Deluxe Reversible Rack in the lower position, then place the rack in the pot. Place the chicken on the rack.

**6.** Slide the Deluxe Layer through the lower layer's handles. Place the polenta slices on the Deluxe layer.

**7.** Close the lid and move the slider to STEAMCRISP. Select STEAM & CRISP, set the temperature to 450°F, and set the time to 10 minutes. Press START/STOP to begin cooking (PrE will display for about 15 minutes as the unit steams, then the timer will start counting down).

**8.** When cooking is complete, carefully remove the rack layer with the polenta, then the rack layer with the chicken.

**9.** Move the slider to AIR FRY/STOVETOP. Select SEAR/SAUTÉ and set the temperature to HI-5. Press START/STOP to begin cooking. Add the butter to the pot and slowly whisk it into the sauce. When the butter is fully incorporated, add the heavy cream and season with salt and pepper. Stir to combine. Cook for about 1 minute.

**10.** When cooking is complete, serve the chicken with the polenta cakes and top with sauce and parsley.

**Per serving:** *Calories: 835; Total Fat: 25g; Saturated Fat: 11g; Cholesterol: 297mg; Sodium: 970mg; Carbohydrates: 35g; Fiber: 2g; Protein: 102g*

# Honey Mustard Chicken Thighs, Garlic Green Beans, and Rice Pilaf

**SERVES 4**

*Honey mustard is my favorite condiment—as a dipper for chicken fingers or French fries. But it's even better when brushed on top of chicken thighs in a three-layer meal. With SteamCrisp™ technology, this meal is out-of-this-world delicious, because the steam helps keep the dark meat succulent, and the crisping gives the ultimate texture to the chicken skin.* —by Meg Jordan

**GLUTEN-FREE**
**NUT-FREE**
**STEAMCRISP MEALS**

**Prep Time:** 10 minutes
**Total Cook Time:**
30 minutes
**Steam:** about 15 minutes
**Cook:** 15 minutes

**Accessories:** Deluxe Reversible Rack (both layers)

2 (12-ounce) boxes rice pilaf, plus ingredients called for in box instructions
Kosher salt
Freshly ground black pepper

1 (12-ounce) bag trimmed green beans
2 tablespoons canola oil
3 garlic cloves, minced
4 (8-ounce) bone-in, skin-on chicken thighs
¼ cup honey mustard

**1.** Put the rice and ingredients called for in the box instructions in the pot and stir until combined. Season with salt and pepper.

**2.** Place the bottom layer of the Deluxe Reversible Rack in the lower position, then place the rack in the pot over the rice mixture.

**3.** In a large bowl, toss the green beans with the oil and garlic, and season with salt and pepper. Lay a 15-inch-long sheet of aluminum foil on a flat surface. Put the beans in the center and fold the edges of the foil in to create a sealed packet. Place the foil packet on the bottom layer of the Deluxe Reversible Rack in the lower position.

**4.** Season the chicken thighs with salt and pepper. Slide the Deluxe Layer through the lower layer's handles. Place the chicken thighs on the Deluxe Layer.

**5.** Close the lid and move the slider to STEAMCRISP. Select STEAM & CRISP, set the temperature to 390°F, and set the time to 15 minutes. Press START/STOP to begin cooking (PrE will display for about 15 minutes as the unit steams, then the timer will start counting down).

**6.** When the timer reads 4 minutes, open the lid and brush the honey mustard on the top of the chicken thighs. Close the lid and continue cooking.

**7.** When cooking is complete, carefully remove the rack with the chicken and green beans. Stir the rice with a wooden spoon or silicone-tipped utensil. Serve the rice with the chicken and green beans.

**Per serving:** *Calories: 1,042; Total Fat: 42g; Saturated Fat: 10g; Cholesterol: 189mg; Sodium: 1,872mg; Carbohydrates: 116g; Fiber: 7g; Protein: 49g*

# Chicken Fajitas

**SERVES 4**

*My family loves making fajitas, because it's the perfect dish to personalize for every-one's taste. I always think of fajitas as being a hassle to make, but with the Ninja® Foodi® SmartLid™, everything is contained in one pot, which keeps prep simple. Enjoy these fajitas with corn or flour tortillas, fresh cilantro, and lime.* —by Kara Bleday

DAIRY-FREE
GLUTEN-FREE
NUT-FREE
STEAMCRISP MEALS

**Prep Time:** 10 minutes
**Total Cook Time:**
26 minutes
**Steam:** about 16 minutes
**Cook:** 10 minutes

**Accessories:** Ninja® Multi-Purpose Pan or 8-inch round pan, Deluxe Reversible Rack (both layers)

**LEVEL 1 (BOTTOM OF POT)**
1 (6- to 8-ounce) package dry Spanish Rice mix, plus the water called for in the box instructions

**LEVEL 2 (BOTTOM LAYER OF RACK)**
1½ pounds boneless chicken breast, cut into 1-inch-thick slices

1 teaspoon kosher salt

1 teaspoon garlic powder

⅛ teaspoon ground cinnamon

2 tablespoons chopped fresh cilantro

¼ teaspoon ground cumin

Grated zest of 1 lime

Juice of 1 lime

**LEVEL 3 (TOP LAYER OF RACK)**
1 small red bell pepper, seeded and quartered

1 small yellow bell pepper, seeded and quartered

1 white onion, quartered

Kosher salt

Freshly ground black pepper

Fixings and toppings (optional)

8 flour tortillas (optional)

Cilantro

Avocado

Sour cream

Lime wedges

**1.** Put the rice and water in the pot and stir until combined.

**2.** In a large bowl, combine the chicken, salt, garlic powder, cinnamon, cilantro, cumin, lime zest, and lime juice and toss to evenly coat. Transfer the seasoned chicken to the Multi-Purpose Pan. Place the pan on the bottom layer of the Deluxe Reversible Rack in the lower position, then place the rack in the pot.

**3.** Slide the Deluxe Layer through the lower layer's handles. Place all the Level 3 ingredients on the Deluxe Layer. It is okay if the pieces overlap, because they will decrease in size as they cook.

**4.** Close the lid and move the slider to STEAMCRISP. Select STEAM & CRISP, set the temperature to 425°F, and set the time to 10 minutes. Press START/STOP to begin cooking (PrE will display for about 16 minutes as the unit steams, then the timer will start counting down).

**5.** When cooking is complete, carefully remove the rack layers. Slice the cooked vegetables and set aside.

**6.** Stir the rice and leave it in the pot, uncovered. If there is water remaining in the pot, move the slider to the right position, select SEAR/SAUTÉ, and cook for 3 to 5 minutes or until all the water has been absorbed.

**7.** Assemble the fajitas with chicken, peppers, onions, and toppings of your choice. Serve with the rice.

**Per serving:** *Calories: 675; Total Fat: 23g; Saturated Fat: 6g; Cholesterol: 109mg; Sodium: 1,305mg; Carbohydrates: 69g; Fiber: 5g; Protein: 46g*

**Variation Tip:**
When cooked in the Multi-Purpose Pan, the chicken will be tender and soft. Switch up the texture by placing the vegetables directly on the second level rack, which will allow the chicken to brown a bit on the top level (without the Multi-Purpose Pan).

# Creamy Chicken Pasta

## SERVES 4 TO 6

*The Ninja® Foodi® SmartLid™ has amazing capabilities with its new SteamCrisp™ technology, but it's also great for those classic pressure cooker favorites. By using the SEAR/SAUTÉ function, you can easily brown your favorite veggies and meat prior to adding pasta for a delicious meal the whole family will love. Not a fan of vodka sauce? Swap it for Alfredo sauce for a new take.* —by Meg Jordan

**NUT-FREE**

**Prep Time:** 10 minutes
**Total Cook Time:**
28 minutes
**Sear/Sauté:** 7 minutes
**Pressure Build:** about
15 minutes
**Cook:** 6 minutes
**Pressure Release:**
10 minutes

2 tablespoons canola oil

1½ pounds boneless,
skinless chicken breasts,
cut into 1-inch pieces

Kosher salt

Freshly ground
black pepper

1 tablespoon garlic powder

1 tablespoon dried oregano

1 (16-ounce) box
penne pasta

3 cups chicken stock

2 (24-ounce) jars
vodka pasta sauce

1 cup grated
Parmesan cheese

1. Close the lid and move the slide to AIR FRY/STOVETOP. Select SEAR/SAUTÉ and set the temperature to 4. Open the lid and select START/STOP to begin preheating. Allow the unit to preheat for 5 minutes.

2. Once the unit is preheated, pour the oil into the pot. When the oil is hot, add the chicken and season with salt and pepper. Cook for about 7 minutes, stirring occasionally, until the chicken is lightly browned.

3. Add the garlic powder, oregano, pasta, chicken stock, and pasta sauce to the pot and stir to combine.

**4.** Close the lid and move the slider to PRESSURE. Make sure the pressure release valve is in the SEAL position. The temperature will default to HIGH, which is the correct setting. Set the time to 6 minutes. Select START/STOP to begin cooking (the unit will build pressure for about 15 minutes before cooking begins).

**5.** When cooking is complete, select KEEP WARM and naturally release the pressure for 10 minutes. Quick release any remaining pressure by turning the pressure release valve to the VENT position. Once all the pressure is released, move the slider to AIR FRY/STOVETOP to unlock the lid, then carefully open it.

**6.** Add the Parmesan cheese, then stir the pasta carefully with a wooden spoon. Serve immediately.

**Per serving:** *Calories: 1,057; Total Fat: 43g; Saturated Fat: 17g; Cholesterol: 207mg; Sodium: 1,486mg; Carbohydrates: 103g; Fiber: 7g; Protein: 65g*

# Chicken Teriyaki Lettuce Wraps

**SERVES 4 TO 6**

*During the week my fiancé and I try to eat slightly healthier than we do on the weekends, when it's full steam ahead on pizza, sandwiches, and fried food. An easy swap to make for sandwiches or tacos is using lettuce instead of bread. Is it always as good? That's debatable, but we're trying here. However, when the lettuce is filled with sweet and delicious pulled chicken teriyaki, you definitely don't miss the carbs. The SmartLid™ does an amazing job of pressure cooking the chicken until tender to make this meal quick, easy, and delicious.* —by Michelle Boland

---

DAIRY-FREE
NUT-FREE

---

**Prep Time:** 10 minutes
**Total Cook Time:**
35 minutes
**Pressure Build:** about
15 minutes
**Pressure Cook:** 20 minutes
**Pressure Release:** Quick

---

**Variation Tip:** Don't love teriyaki? Try another prepared sauce, such as Buffalo, sesame-ginger, lemon-garlic, or any other marinade you like.

---

**Per serving:** *Calories: 403; Total Fat: 9g; Saturated Fat: 3g; Cholesterol: 213mg; Sodium: 2,110mg; Carbohydrates: 23g; Fiber: 1g; Protein: 53g*

---

1 (14-ounce) bottle
  prepared teriyaki sauce

1 cup chicken stock

2 pounds boneless,
  skinless chicken thighs

1 head Bibb lettuce,
  leaves separated

¼ cup diced fresh
  pineapple

¼ cup sliced scallions,
  white and green parts

Radishes, thinly
  sliced, as desired

Sesame seeds, as desired

**1.** Combine the teriyaki sauce, chicken stock, and chicken thighs in the bottom of the pot and stir.

**2.** Close the lid and move the slider to PRESSURE. Make sure the pressure release valve is in the SEAL position. The temperature will default to HIGH, which is the correct setting. Set the time to 20 minutes. Select START/STOP to begin cooking (the unit will build pressure for about 15 minutes before the timer starts counting down).

**3.** When cooking is complete, select KEEP WARM and quick release the pressure by turning the pressure release valve to the VENT position. Once the pressure is released, move the slider to AIR FRY/STOVETOP to unlock the lid, then carefully open it.

**4.** Carefully shred the chicken using silicone-tipped tongs. Assemble the lettuce wraps using 1 piece of Bibb lettuce per wrap and layering shredded chicken, pineapple, scallions, radishes, and a sprinkle of sesame seeds.

# Butter Cracker Chicken Tenders with Creamy Pasta, Broccoli, and Cauliflower

**SERVES 4**

*This easy and fast meal will please even the pickiest eaters. Being able to cook a starch, vegetable, and protein all in one unit is revolutionary and will be a huge win for your family. And not only do you get to put a delicious, well-rounded meal on the table in half an hour, you will have very few dishes to clean up later.*
—by Michelle Boland

**NUT-FREE
STEAMCRISP MEALS**

**Prep Time:** 10 minutes
**Total Cook Time:**
21 minutes
**Steam:** 11 minutes
**Cook:** 10 minutes

**Accessories:** Deluxe Reversible Rack (both layers)

**LEVEL 1 (BOTTOM OF POT)**

1 (16-ounce) box pasta, such as ziti or gemelli

1 (15-ounce) jar Alfredo sauce

3 cups chicken stock

1 cup whole milk

**LEVEL 2 (BOTTOM LAYER OF RACK)**

1 (12-ounce) bag broccoli and cauliflower florets

1 tablespoon canola oil

Kosher salt

Freshly ground black pepper

**LEVEL 3 (TOP LAYER OF RACK)**

¼ cup all-purpose flour

Kosher salt

Freshly ground black pepper

1 large egg

1 cup crushed butter crackers

8 fresh chicken tenders

1. Put the pasta, stock, and milk in the pot and stir to combine.

2. In a medium bowl, toss together all the broccoli and cauliflower and oil and season with salt and pepper. Lay a 15-inch-long sheet of aluminum foil on a flat surface. Put the vegetables in the center and fold the edges of the foil in to create a sealed packet. Place the foil packet on the bottom layer of the Deluxe Reversible Rack in the lower position, then place the rack in the pot over the pasta mixture.

CONTINUED >

**3.** Prepare the Level 3 ingredients: Create a dredging station by pouring the flour into a medium bowl. Season with salt and pepper. Crack the egg into a separate medium bowl and whisk. Pour the crushed butter crackers into a third medium bowl.

**4.** Dredge one side of each chicken tender in the flour, shaking off any excess flour. Carefully dip the floured side in the egg, then in the butter crackers.

**5.** Slide the Deluxe Layer through the lower layer's handles. Place the chicken, breaded-side up, on the Deluxe Layer.

**6.** Close the lid and move the slider to STEAMCRISP. Select STEAM & CRISP, set the temperature to 390°F, and set the time to 10 minutes. Press START/STOP to begin cooking (PrE will display for about 11 minutes as the unit steams, then the timer will start counting down).

**7.** When cooking is complete, carefully remove the rack layers with the chicken tenders and foil packet. Stir the pasta and serve warm with the chicken tenders and vegetables.

*Per serving: Calories: 1,162; Total Fat: 62g; Saturated Fat: 34g; Cholesterol: 238mg; Sodium: 710mg; Carbohydrates: 108g; Fiber: 6g; Protein: 43g*

# Sun-Dried Tomato Chicken Thighs with Broccoli and Rice

**SERVES 4**

*When I think of sun-dried tomatoes, I immediately think of pasta—the two undeniably go hand in hand. And yet, rice and chicken paired with herby vibrant sun-dried tomatoes is a welcome change. This meal comes together remarkably quickly, and the best part is that it all cooks at the same time. Fluffy rice, broccoli that soaks up some of the sun-dried tomato oil while cooking, and perfectly done chicken is a meal that will please any crowd.* —by Avery Lowe

**GLUTEN-FREE**
**NUT-FREE**
**STEAMCRISP MEALS**

**Prep Time:** 15 minutes
**Total Cook Time:**
20 minutes
**Steam:** about 8 minutes
**Cook:** 12 minutes

**Accessories:** Deluxe
Reversible Rack
(both layers)

**Substitution Tip:** If you'd prefer bone-in chicken breasts instead of chicken thighs, adjust the temperature to 375°F. The cooking time should still be 10 to 15 minutes.

**LEVEL 1 (BOTTOM OF POT)**

2 (6.09-ounce) boxes rice pilaf, plus

4 cups water

ingredients called for in box instructions

**LEVEL 2 (BOTTOM LAYER OF RACK)**

3 heaping cups broccoli florets (about 10 ounces total)

3 tablespoons garlic powder

2 tablespoons extra-virgin olive oil

Kosher salt

Freshly ground black pepper

**LEVEL 3 (TOP LAYER OF RACK)**

4 (6- to 8-ounce) boneless, skinless chicken thighs

Kosher salt

Freshly ground black pepper

¼ cup sun-dried tomatoes in oil, finely minced

¼ cup fresh parsley, minced

1. Start with the Level 3 ingredients: Season the chicken on all sides with salt and pepper. Place in a bowl and evenly cover with the sun-dried tomatoes. Set aside.

2. Prepare the Level 2 ingredients: In a medium bowl, combine the broccoli, garlic powder, and oil. Season with salt and pepper and toss until the broccoli is evenly coated.

*CONTINUED >*

**3.** Prepare the Level 1 ingredients: Put the rice pilaf, ingredients called for in the box instructions, and water in the bottom of the pot.

**4.** Cover the bottom layer of the Deluxe Reversible Rack with a sheet of aluminum foil. Place the rack in the pot. Place the prepared broccoli on top of the foil.

**5.** Slide the Deluxe Layer through the lower layer's handles. Place the chicken thighs and sun-dried tomatoes on the top layer of the rack.

**6.** Close the lid and move the slider to STEAMCRISP. Select STEAM & CRISP, set the temperature to 390°F, and set the time to 12 minutes. Press START/STOP to begin cooking (PrE will display for about 8 minutes as the unit steams, then the timer will start counting down).

**7.** When cooking is complete, remove the rack layers. Stir the rice and serve with the chicken, sun-dried tomatoes, and broccoli. Garnish with the parsley.

**Per serving:** *Calories: 706; Total Fat: 19g; Saturated Fat: 4g; Cholesterol: 213mg; Sodium: 1263mg; Carbohydrates: 77g; Fiber: 6g; Protein: 57g*

# Spiced Grilled Chicken with Pilau Rice

**SERVES 3 TO 4**

*These delicious, gently spiced roast chicken thighs with pilau rice are cooked in under an hour using the simple SteamCrisp one-touch meal system. The chicken is marinated in a curry spice blend and then steamed. This means the chicken remains moist and tender, while the rice absorbs some of the lovely juices. This is a meal the whole family is sure to enjoy.* —by Jennie Vincent

---

**GLUTEN-FREE**
**NUT-FREE**
**STEAMCRISP MEALS**

---

**Prep Time:** 15 minutes, plus 8 hours to marinate
**Total Cook Time:**
46 minutes
**Sear/Sauté:** 6 minutes
**Steam:** about 15 minutes
**Cook:** 25 minutes

---

**Accessories:** Deluxe Reversible Rack (bottom layer only)

### LEVEL 1 (BOTTOM OF POT)

- 2 tablespoons unsalted butter
- 1 white onion, finely chopped
- 1 cinnamon stick
- 4 green cardamom pods (or 2 teaspoons ground green cardamom)
- 2 whole cloves
- 2 teaspoons ground turmeric
- 2 bay leaves
- 2 cups basmati rice, rinsed until water runs clear
- 4 cups water

### LEVEL 2 (BOTTOM LAYER OF RACK)

- 1 cup plain yogurt
- Juice of 1 lemon
- 1 tablespoon canola oil
- 2 teaspoons ground turmeric
- 1 tablespoon garam masala
- 1 teaspoon ground cumin
- 1 teaspoon paprika
- 3 tablespoons tomato paste
- 1 tablespoon grated fresh ginger
- 3 garlic cloves, minced
- Kosher salt
- Freshly ground black pepper
- 6 to 8 (6-ounce) bone-in, skin-on chicken thighs or drumsticks

CONTINUED >

## Spiced Grilled Chicken with Pilau Rice continued

Per serving: Calories: 1,305; Total Fat: 63g; Saturated Fat: 20g; Cholesterol: 309mg; Sodium: 336mg; Carbohydrates: 119g; Fiber: 5g; Protein: 60g

1. Start with the Level 2 ingredients: In a large bowl, combine the yogurt, lemon juice, oil, turmeric, garam masala, cumin, paprika, tomato paste, ginger, and garlic. Season with salt and pepper and whisk together. Place the marinade and chicken in a large resealable plastic bag. Massage the outside of the bag to work the marinade over all parts of the chicken. Place the bag in the refrigerator for at least 8 hours and up to 24 hours to marinate the chicken.

2. After the chicken is marinated, prepare the Level 1 ingredients: Close the lid and move the slider to AIR FRY/STOVETOP. Select SEAR/SAUTÉ and set the temperature to HI-5. Open the lid and select START/STOP to begin preheating. Allow the unit to preheat for 5 minutes.

3. When the unit has preheated, put the butter in the pot. When the butter has melted, add the onion, cinnamon, cardamom, cloves, turmeric, and bay leaves and sauté until the onion has softened, about 6 minutes. Add the rice and water to the pot and stir to combine.

4. Place the bottom layer of the Deluxe Reversible Rack in the lower position, then place the rack in the pot. Remove the chicken thighs from the marinade and pat dry with paper towels. Discard any excess marinade. Place the chicken on the rack.

5. Close the lid and move the slider to STEAMCRISP. Select STEAM & CRISP, set the temperature to 375°F, and set the time to 25 minutes. Press START/STOP to begin cooking (PrE will display for about 15 minutes as the unit steams, then the timer will start counting down).

6. When cooking is complete, carefully remove the rack layer with the chicken. Remove the bay leaves, stir the rice and serve warm with the chicken.

# Chicken Parm with Pasta Primavera

**SERVES 4 TO 6**

*Chicken parm with pasta primavera is one of my favorite weeknight dishes, and with SteamCrisp™ technology, this is a true one-pot, set-it-and-forget-it meal. Plus, it's a great way to pack your meal full of delicious fresh vegetables that taste great with the bright and citrusy cream sauce.* —by Caroline Schliep

**NUT-FREE
STEAMCRISP MEALS**

**Prep Time:** 10 minutes
**Total Cook Time:**
35 minutes
**Steam:** about 20 minutes
**Cook:** 15 minutes

**Accessories:** Deluxe Reversible Rack (both layers)

**Substitution Tip:** The vegetables used in this dish can be swapped out for any vegetables of choice or whatever is in season.

### LEVEL 1 (BOTTOM OF POT)

1 (16-ounce) box cavatappi pasta

4 cups chicken stock

1 tablespoon minced garlic

½ cup heavy (whipping) cream

3 cups grated Parmesan cheese

Grated zest of 1 lemon

Juice of 1 lemon

¼ cup coarsely chopped fresh parsley

### LEVEL 2 (BOTTOM LAYER OF RACK)

1 yellow bell pepper, seeded and cut into thin strips

1 small red onion, cut into ½-inch-thick rounds

1 zucchini, halved lengthwise and cut into ½-inch half-moons

½ bunch asparagus, ends trimmed, halved crosswise

1 cup cherry tomatoes

1 tablespoon canola oil

Kosher salt

Freshly ground black pepper

### LEVEL 3 (TOP LAYER OF RACK)

1 cup all-purpose flour

2 large eggs

1½ cups panko bread crumbs

¼ cup grated Parmesan cheese

4 (6-ounce) thin, boneless, skinless chicken breast cutlets

1. Start with the Level 1 ingredients: Combine the pasta, chicken stock, and garlic in the pot and stir.

2. Place the Level 2 ingredients, the pepper, onion, zucchini, asparagus, cherry tomatoes, and oil in a large bowl. Season with salt and pepper and toss to evenly coat with the oil.

*CONTINUED >*

**Per serving:** *Calories: 1,254; Total Fat: 44g; Saturated Fat: 21g; Cholesterol:254mg;Sodium:1431mg; Carbohydrates: 128g; Fiber: 7g; Protein: 84g*

**3.** Lay a 15-inch-long sheet of aluminum foil on a flat surface. Put the vegetable mixture in the center and fold the edges of the foil in to create a sealed packet. Place the foil packet on the bottom layer of the Deluxe Reversible Rack in the lower position, then place the rack in the pot over the pasta mixture.

**4.** Cover the top layer of the Deluxe Reversible Rack with another sheet of foil, then slide it through the lower layer's handles.

**5.** Prepare the Level 3 ingredients: Create a dredging station by pouring the flour into a medium bowl. Crack the eggs into a separate medium bowl and whisk. In a third medium bowl, combine the bread crumbs and Parmesan.

**6.** Dredge each chicken cutlet in the flour, shaking off any excess flour. Dip in the eggs, then in the bread crumb mixture, evenly coating both sides. Place the chicken on the foil on the top layer of the rack.

**7.** Close the lid and move the slider to STEAMCRISP. Select STEAM & CRISP, set the temperature to 390ºF, and set the time to 15 minutes. Press START/STOP to begin cooking (PrE will display for about 20 minutes as the unit steams, then the timer will start counting down).

**8.** After 7 minutes, open the lid and flip the chicken. Close the lid to continue cooking.

**9.** When cooking is complete, carefully remove the entire rack with the chicken and foil packet and set aside. Add the cream, Parmesan, lemon zest and juice, and parsley from the Level 1 ingredients, plus the vegetables from the foil packet, to the pasta and stir to combine. Serve the pasta with the chicken cutlets.

**Honey Mustard Crusted Pork with Brussels Sprouts and Creamy Scallion Rice,** *page 162*

# 8

# Beef, Pork, and Lamb Main Dishes

# Barbecue Kielbasa with Crispy Broccoli and Mac 'n' Cheese

**SERVES 4**

*My favorite part of the Ninja® Foodi® SmartLid™ is the ability to get a plate of food with not just a variety of flavors but also a variety of textures. What would normally take me two pans and an oven just takes one pot. By placing the broccoli on the top of the Deluxe Reversible Rack, you're able to achieve a crispy, flavorful vegetable without preheating your oven. That's what makes these meals stand out!*
—by Kara Bleday

**NUT-FREE**
**STEAMCRISP MEALS**

**Prep Time:** 5 minutes
**Total Cook Time:**
22 minutes
**Steam:** about 12 minutes
**Cook:** 10 minutes

**Accessories:** Deluxe Reversible Rack (both layers)

**LEVEL 1 (BOTTOM OF POT)**
2 cups vegetable stock
1¼ cups whole milk

2 (6-ounce) boxes mac and cheese and cheese packets
2 tablespoons unsalted butter

**LEVEL 2 (BOTTOM LAYER OF RACK)**
1 (14-ounce) kielbasa

½ cup prepared barbecue sauce

**LEVEL 3 (TOP LAYER OF RACK)**
3 heaping cups broccoli florets (about 10 ounces total)
1 tablespoon extra-virgin olive oil

Kosher salt
Freshly ground black pepper

1. Start with the Level 1 ingredients: Combine the vegetable stock, milk, and pasta (set the cheese packets aside until step 8) in the pot and stir.

2. Prepare the Level 2 ingredients: Slice the kielbasa in half lengthwise almost all the way through and open it like a book. Brush with the barbecue sauce on all sides.

3. In a large bowl, combine the broccoli and oil. Season with salt and pepper and toss to evenly coat the broccoli.

**4.** Place the bottom layer of the Deluxe Reversible Rack in the lower position, then place the rack in the pot. Place the sausage on the rack.

**5.** Slide the Deluxe Layer through the lower layer's handles. Place the broccoli on the Deluxe Layer.

**6.** Close the lid and move the slider to STEAMCRISP. Select STEAM & CRISP, set the temperature to 370°F, and set the time to 10 minutes. Press START/STOP to begin cooking (PrE will display for about 12 minutes as the unit steams, then the timer will start counting down).

**7.** When cooking is complete, carefully remove the rack with the broccoli and kielbasa.

**8.** Add the cheese packets and butter (Level 1 ingredients) to the cooked pasta and stir until the butter has melted and the cheese is evenly combined. Serve warm with the kielbasa and broccoli.

**Per serving:** *Calories: 811; Total Fat: 34g; Saturated Fat: 13g; Cholesterol: 92mg; Sodium: 2,225mg; Carbohydrates: 91g; Fiber: 7g; Protein: 26g*

**Substitution Tip:**
Hot dogs are a great substitute here if you have picky eaters at home. Use 3 or 4 hot dogs and cut 3 to 4 small slits in the top of each hot dog. The cook time is the same.

# Honey Mustard Crusted Pork with Brussels Sprouts and Creamy Scallion Rice

**SERVES 4**

*This dish came together quickly as I prepped for this cookbook. The pairing of pork and mustard is one of my favorites, and for some reason I always reach for Brussels sprouts when serving pork. The rice is something I make for my fiancée, Michelle, who is obsessed with rice, sour cream, and cheese, so it was kind of a no-brainer side dish. The perfect finishing touch for this dish would be a nice dollop of applesauce on the side, to help round out this delicious meal.*

—by Craig White

**NUT-FREE
STEAMCRISP MEALS**

**Prep Time:** 10 minutes
**Total Cook Time:**
30 minutes
**Steam:** about 20 minutes
**Cook:** 10 minutes

**Accessories:** Deluxe
Reversible Rack
(both layers)

### LEVEL 1 (BOTTOM OF POT)
- 2 cups white rice
- 4 cups chicken stock
- Kosher salt
- Freshly ground black pepper
- ½ cup sour cream
- 1 cup shredded cheddar cheese
- 3 scallions, thinly sliced

### LEVEL 2 (BOTTOM LAYER OF RACK)
- 1 pound Brussels sprouts, outer leaves removed, halved lengthwise
- 1 tablespoon canola oil
- Kosher salt
- Freshly ground black pepper

### LEVEL 3 (TOP LAYER OF RACK)
- 4 (6- to 8-ounce) boneless pork chops
- Kosher salt
- Freshly ground black pepper
- 2 tablespoons honey mustard
- ¼ cup garlic and herb bread crumbs

1. Start with the Level 1 ingredients: Combine the rice and chicken stock in the pot. Season with salt and pepper and stir.

**2.** Place the bottom layer of the Deluxe Reversible Rack in the lower position, cover with a sheet of aluminum foil, and place the rack in the pot.

**3.** Prepare the Level 2 ingredients: In a large bowl, combine the Brussels sprouts and oil. Season with salt and pepper and toss until the sprouts are evenly coated. Place the Brussels sprouts on the foil.

**4.** Prepare the Level 3 ingredients: Season the pork chops with salt and pepper on both sides. Rub the top of each chop with the honey mustard, then top with the bread crumbs, pressing to help them stick.

**5.** Slide the Deluxe Layer through the lower layer's handles. Place the pork chops on the Deluxe Layer.

**6.** Close the lid and move the slider to STEAMCRISP. Select STEAM & CRISP, set the temperature to 390°F, and set the time to 10 minutes. Press START/STOP to begin cooking (PrE will display for about 20 minutes as the unit steams, then the timer will start counting down).

**7.** When cooking is complete, carefully remove the rack layers. Add the sour cream, cheddar cheese, and scallions (Level 1 ingredients) to the pot with the rice, stir to combine, and season with salt and pepper. Serve the rice with the pork chops and Brussels sprouts.

**Variation Tip:** Don't have honey mustard? Use ranch dressing instead.

**Per serving:** *Calories: 924; Total Fat: 28g; Saturated Fat: 12g; Cholesterol: 193mg; Sodium: 589mg; Carbohydrates: 95g; Fiber: 7g; Protein: 70g*

# Marinated Pork Chops with Apples and Onions

**SERVES 4**

*Sous vide is a style of cooking in which food is gently cooked in a temperature-controlled water bath. It has become more popular in the last few years, which is why we've incorporated the function into the Ninja® Foodi® SmartLid™. Sous vide cooking works especially well with proteins, followed up by a quick pan sear for the ultimate texture sensation. The sweet and slightly spicy sauce pairs so well with the pork and apples. If you happen to have calvados (an apple liqueur) on hand, feel free to use that in place of the wine for a heightened apple flavor.* —by Melissa Celli

DAIRY-FREE
GLUTEN-FREE
NUT-FREE

**Prep Time:** 5 minutes
**Total Cook Time:** 2 hours 20 minutes
**Sous vide:** 2 hours
**Sear/Sauté:** 20 minutes

- 2 tablespoons freshly squeezed lemon juice
- ¼ cup plus 1 tablespoon canola oil, divided
- ½ cup maple syrup
- 2 teaspoons apple cider vinegar
- 2 tablespoons Dijon mustard
- 1 teaspoon smoked paprika
- 1 teaspoon minced garlic
- 1 teaspoon kosher salt
- ½ teaspoon freshly ground black pepper
- ¼ teaspoon cayenne pepper
- 4 (6- to 7-ounce) boneless pork chops
- 1 medium white onion, sliced
- 4 rosemary sprigs
- 12 cups room temperature water, plus 1 tablespoon
- 3 Honeycrisp, Pink Lady, or Gala apples, thinly sliced
- ¼ cup white wine
- 1 tablespoon cornstarch

1. In a large bowl, prepare the marinade by whisking together the lemon juice, ¼ cup of oil, maple syrup, vinegar, mustard, paprika, garlic, salt, black pepper, and cayenne pepper.

2. Into each of two large resealable bags, put 2 pork chops, half of the onion, 2 rosemary sprigs, and half of the marinade. Tightly seal both bags.

**3.** Fill the pot with 12 cups of water.

**4.** Close the lid and move the slider to AIR FRY/ STOVETOP. Select SOUS VIDE, set the temperature to 145ºF, and set the time to 2 hours. Press START/STOP to begin preheating.

**5.** When the unit has preheated, place each bag in the pot using the water displacement method: Partially zip the seal on the bag, then place the bottom of the bag in the water, gently massaging out the air surrounding the pork chops. The pressure of the water will force all the air out of the bag as you slowly submerge it. When the water level is just below the zip-line of the bag, completely seal the bag. Ensure the bags are fully zipped so no water can enter during cooking. Close the lid to begin cooking.

**6.** After 2 hours, open the lid, remove one bag, open it, and check the internal temperature of the pork chops using an instant-read thermometer. The internal temperature should be 145ºF or above. Once the temperature has been reached, remove both bags from the pot.

**7.** Carefully remove the pot and discard the water. Return the pot to the unit. Select SEAR/SAUTÉ and set the temperature to HI-5. Select START/STOP to begin preheating. Allow the unit to preheat for 5 minutes.

**Substitution Tip:** If the apples listed are not available in your area, use another type of apple appropriate for baking and cooking, such as Jonagold or Braeburn apples. For a tarter flavor, use green or Granny Smith apples.

*CONTINUED >*

8. When the unit has preheated, pour the remaining 1 tablespoon of oil into the pot. Remove the pork chops from the bag and gently pat dry with paper towels. Set the marinade aside for the moment. When the oil is hot, add the pork chops to the pot and sear for about 5 minutes. Flip the pork chops and add the onion from the marinade to the pot. Discard the rosemary and reserve the marinade. Cook the pork chops for 5 minutes more, until an instant-read thermometer reads 145°F. Remove the chops and set aside to rest.

9. Add the apples to the onion and sauté for 5 minutes, stirring frequently. Add the white wine and gently scrape up any browned bits on the bottom of the pot. Add the reserved marinade and bring to a boil.

10. In a small bowl, stir together the cornstarch and remaining 1 tablespoon of water. Add the cornstarch mixture to the boiling sauce mixture and whisk until combined and thickened, about 30 seconds.

11. When cooking is complete, slice the pork chops and top with the apples, onions, and sauce.

*Per serving: Calories: 484; Total Fat: 19g; Saturated Fat: 5g; Cholesterol: 114mg; Sodium: 276mg; Carbohydrates: 38g; Fiber: 4g; Protein: 38g*

# Korean-Style Sticky Ribs

**SERVES 2**

*The perfect crowd-pleaser in an hour? No, you're not imagining it. By using pressure cooking combined with air frying, you can prepare these delicious, sweet, spicy, sticky ribs in no time at all. Pressure cooking the ribs means they cook quickly while maintaining their tenderness, and air frying finishes them off to perfection. These tender, melt-in-your-mouth ribs have so much flavor that you'll be asked for them again and again.* —by Jennie Vincent

DAIRY-FREE
NUT-FREE

**Prep Time:** 15 minutes
**Total Cook Time:**
46 minutes
**Pressure Build:** about
6 minutes
**Pressure Cook:** 25 minutes
**Pressure Release:**
5 minutes
**Air fry:** 10 minutes

**Accessories:** Deluxe Reversible Rack (bottom layer only)

- 1 tablespoon gochugaru powder or red pepper flakes
- 1 tablespoon sweet paprika
- 5 garlic cloves, minced, divided
- Kosher salt
- Freshly ground black pepper
- 1 pound pork spareribs

- 1 cup water
- 4 tablespoons gochujang paste or sriracha
- 4 tablespoons ketchup
- 2 tablespoons soy sauce
- 2 tablespoons honey
- 1 tablespoon light brown sugar
- 1 tablespoon grated fresh ginger
- 4 scallions, sliced, for garnish

1. In a large bowl, combine the gochugaru powder, paprika, and two-fifths of the garlic. Season with salt and pepper. Add the ribs and evenly coat the ribs with the dry rub.

2. Pour the water into the pot and add the ribs.

3. Close the lid and move the slider to PRESSURE. Make sure the pressure release valve is in the SEAL position. The temperature will default to HIGH, which is the correct setting. Set the time to 25 minutes. Select START/STOP to begin cooking (the unit will build pressure for about 6 minutes before cooking begins).

*CONTINUED >*

4. While the ribs cook, prepare the glaze. In a large bowl, whisk together the gochujang paste, ketchup, soy sauce, honey, brown sugar, remaining three-fifths of the garlic, and the ginger.

5. When cooking is complete, select KEEP WARM, then allow the pressure to release naturally for 5 minutes. Release the remaining pressure by turning the pressure release valve to the VENT position. When the pressure has released, move the slider to AIR FRY/STOVETOP to unlock the lid, then carefully open it.

6. Transfer the ribs to the glaze and toss to evenly coat.

7. Place the bottom layer of the Deluxe Reversible Rack in the lower position, then place the rack in the pot. Place the ribs on the rack.

8. Close the lid. Select AIR FRY, set the temperature to 400°F, and set the time to 10 minutes. Select START/STOP to begin cooking.

9. When cooking is complete, remove the ribs and brush with any remaining glaze. Top with the scallions and serve warm.

**Per serving:** *Calories: 828; Total Fat: 53g; Saturated Fat: 17g; Cholesterol: 181mg; Sodium: 1,632mg; Carbohydrates: 48g; Fiber: 5g; Protein: 39g*

# Marinated Pork Tenderloin, Lemon Rice, Squash, and Asparagus

**SERVES 2 TO 3**

*During the week, life can be busy, and getting creative with ingredients and preparing an interesting meal for the family can be a challenge. By using the brilliant SteamCrisp one-touch meal system, making an entire meal is now a breeze. This recipe is a gorgeous combination of flavorsome, juicy pork tenderloin, with sweet squash and fresh, steamed asparagus, all done in under an hour.* —by Jennie Vincent

DAIRY-FREE
GLUTEN-FREE
NUT-FREE
STEAMCRISP MEALS

**Prep Time:** 15 minutes
**Total Cook Time:**
43 minutes
**Steam:** about 15 minutes
**Cook:** 28 minutes

**Accessories:** Deluxe
Reversible Rack
(both layers)

**LEVEL 1 (BOTTOM OF POT)**

2 cups basmati rice

4 cups chicken broth

Juice of 1 lemon

**LEVEL 2 (BOTTOM LAYER OF RACK)**

2 tablespoons
   Dijon mustard

Juice of 1 lemon

2 garlic cloves, minced

2 tablespoons honey

1 teaspoon smoked paprika

Kosher salt

Freshly ground
   black pepper

1 (1½-pound) boneless
   pork tenderloin

1 pound butternut
   squash, peeled and
   cut into 1-inch pieces

1 tablespoon extra-virgin
   olive oil

**LEVEL 3 (TOP LAYER OF RACK)**
1 bunch asparagus, trimmed

1. Start with the Level 1 ingredients: Combine the rice, chicken broth, and lemon juice in the pot and stir.

2. Prepare the Level 2 ingredients: In a small bowl, combine the mustard, lemon juice, garlic, honey, and paprika. Season with salt and pepper. Evenly brush the pork tenderloin with the mustard mixture.

3. In a large bowl, combine the squash and oil. Season with salt and pepper and toss until the squash is evenly coated.

**4.** Prepare the Level 3 ingredients: Lay a 15-inch-long sheet of aluminum foil on a flat surface. Put the asparagus in the center and fold the edges of the foil in to create a sealed packet.

**5.** Place the bottom layer of the Deluxe Reversible Rack in the lower position, and cover with a sheet of foil, then place the rack in the pot. Place the pork tenderloin on top of the rack, then surround it with the squash.

**6.** Slide the Deluxe Layer through the lower layer's handles. Place the foil packet on the Deluxe Layer.

**7.** Close the lid and move the slider to STEAMCRISP. Select STEAM & CRISP, set the temperature to 375°F, and set the time to 28 minutes. Press START/STOP to begin cooking (PrE will display for about 15 minutes as the unit steams, then the timer will start counting down).

**8.** When cooking is complete, carefully remove the entire rack with the asparagus and pork tenderloin. Allow the pork tenderloin to rest for 5 minutes before slicing.

**9.** Stir the rice and serve it with the pork tenderloin, asparagus, and squash.

**Substitution Tip:** If you don't want asparagus, simply substitute a green vegetable of your choice.

*Per serving: Calories: 1,247; Total Fat: 17g; Saturated Fat: 4g; Cholesterol: 147mg; Sodium: 383mg; Carbohydrates: 208g; Fiber: 11g; Protein: 65g*

# Pasta with Homemade Sauce and Meatballs

**SERVES 4 TO 6**

*How can you go wrong with pasta and meatballs for dinner? This dish is super simple to make, and the homemade vodka sauce just adds an extra special element to this recipe. Also, with the help of SteamCrisp™ technology, the meatballs come out super tender and juicy on the inside yet have a nice char on the exterior. This dish makes a great addition to your weekly meal rotation.* —by Caroline Schliep

**NUT-FREE**
**STEAMCRISP MEALS**

**Prep Time:** 10 minutes
**Total Cook Time:**
40 minutes
**Sear/Sauté:** 5 minutes
**Steam:** about 20 minutes
**Cook:** 15 minutes

**Accessories:** Deluxe Reversible Rack (bottom layer only)

**LEVEL 1 (BOTTOM OF POT)**

1 tablespoon canola oil

1 medium white onion, diced

1 tablespoon minced garlic

2 teaspoons red pepper flakes

Kosher salt

Freshly ground black pepper

¼ cup vodka

1 (16-ounce) box penne pasta

2 (28-ounce) cans crushed tomatoes

¾ cup heavy (whipping) cream

**LEVEL 2 (TOP LAYER OF RACK)**

1 cup seasoned panko bread crumbs

⅔ cup whole milk

1½ pounds ground pork

1½ pounds ground beef

¼ cup grated Parmesan cheese

¼ cup chopped fresh parsley

Kosher salt

Freshly ground black pepper

Nonstick cooking spray

**1.** Start with the Level 2 ingredients: To make the meatballs, in a medium bowl combine the bread crumbs and milk and stir. Allow the mixture to sit for 5 minutes, then add the pork, beef, Parmesan cheese, and parsley. Season with salt and pepper and evenly combine. Form the mixture into 24 (1-inch-round) meatballs. Place the meatballs on a plate or platter and place in the refrigerator while you prepare the sauce.

**2.** Prepare the Level 1 ingredients: Close the lid and move the slider to AIR FRY/STOVETOP. Select SEAR/SAUTÉ and set the temperature to HI-5. Open the lid and select START/STOP to begin preheating. Allow the unit to preheat for 5 minutes.

**3.** When the unit has preheated, combine the oil, onion, garlic, and red pepper flakes in the pot. Season with salt and pepper and cook, stirring frequently, until the onion is tender, about 5 minutes.

**4.** Add the vodka and gently scrape up any browned bits from the bottom of the pot. Add the pasta and tomatoes and stir to combine. Press START/STOP to stop cooking.

**5.** Place the bottom layer of the Deluxe Reversible Rack in the higher position and cover with a sheet of aluminum foil. Spray the foil with cooking spray, then place the rack in the pot. Remove the meatballs from the refrigerator and place them on the foil.

**6.** Close the lid and move the slider to STEAMCRISP. Select STEAM & CRISP, set the temperature to 390°F, and set the time to 15 minutes. Press START/STOP to begin cooking (PrE will display for about 20 minutes as the unit steams, then the timer will start counting down).

**7.** After 7 minutes, open the lid and flip the meatballs. Close the lid to continue cooking.

**8.** When cooking is complete, carefully remove the rack with the meatballs and set aside. Stir the cream into the pasta and serve with the meatballs.

**Hack It:** For simpler prep, you could use two (24-ounce) jars of premade pasta sauce and frozen premade meatballs instead of making them yourself. Pour the sauce into the pot, then pick up the recipe in step 5. The frozen meatballs do not need to be thawed before cooking.

*Per serving: Calories: 1,555; Total Fat: 71g; Saturated Fat: 30g; Cholesterol: 299mg; Sodium: 1241mg; Carbohydrates: 131g; Fiber: 12g; Protein: 93g*

# Shepherd's Pie

*Shepherd's pie is one of my ultimate comfort foods, but it involves many steps to get to the final product. By using one vessel to cook everything, this labor-intensive meal becomes a quick weeknight reliable. Using instant mashed potatoes eliminates a large chunk of the process, without eliminating any flavor. The mashed potatoes are baked again in the final step with pats of butter to brown and enrich them even further.* —by Avery Lowe

**GLUTEN-FREE**
**NUT-FREE**
**STEAMCRISP MEALS**

**Prep Time:** 10 minutes
**Total Cook Time:**
33 minutes
**Sear/Sauté:** 25 minutes
**Bake/Roast:** 8 minutes

- 1 (13.75-ounce) box instant mashed potatoes
- 2 tablespoons canola oil
- 1 yellow or white onion, finely diced
- 2 garlic cloves, minced
- 2 teaspoons fresh thyme or 1 teaspoon dried
- 1 pound ground beef
- Kosher salt
- Freshly ground black pepper
- 1 (12-ounce) bag frozen peas and carrots
- 2 tablespoons tomato paste
- 2 tablespoons Worcestershire sauce
- 1½ cups beef broth
- 3 tablespoons unsalted butter, cut into pieces

1. Prepare the mashed potatoes for 8 servings following the box instructions.

2. Close the lid and move the slider to AIR FRY/STOVETOP. Select SEAR/SAUTÉ and set the temperature to 4. Open the lid and select START/STOP to begin preheating. Pour the oil into the pot.

3. When the oil is shimmering, add the onion and garlic and cook, stirring frequently, for 2 minutes. Add the thyme and cook until fragrant, about 30 seconds. Add the beef and season with salt and pepper. Cook, stirring often, until the beef is cooked through, about 5 minutes.

4. Add the frozen peas and carrots and let them heat through. Stir in the tomato paste and Worcestershire sauce and cook for 2 more minutes.

5. Add the beef broth. Bring to a simmer and cook until the mixture begins to thicken, about 13 minutes.

6. Add the mashed potatoes on top in an even layer. Top with the pieces of butter.

7. Press START/STOP to reset the unit. Select BAKE/ROAST, set the temperature to 375°F, and set the time to 8 minutes. Select START/STOP to begin cooking.

8. When cooking is complete, serve immediately.

**Per serving:** *Calories: 423; Total Fat: 21g; Saturated Fat: 5g; Cholesterol: 51mg; Sodium: 497mg; Carbohydrates: 42g; Fiber: 6g; Protein: 18g*

# Barbecue Marinated Steak Tips with Corn on the Cob and Yellow Rice

**SERVES 4**

*This dish of marinated steak tips, yellow rice, and roasted corn on the cob reminds me of Fourth of July barbecues with my family. It's a very nostalgic, comforting meal for me. The fact that all this food can be made with little fuss is impressive and comes in handy when you're cooking for a hungry family. The trick to this meal is marinating the steak the morning of or the day before; that way, when you're ready to make dinner, the meat will already be seasoned and ready to go.*

—by Myles Bryan

**DAIRY-FREE**
**GLUTEN-FREE**
**NUT-FREE**
**STEAMCRISP MEALS**

**Prep Time:** 10 minutes, plus 6 hours to marinate
**Total Cook Time:** 23 minutes
**Steam:** about 18 minutes
**Cook:** 5 minutes

**Accessories:** Deluxe Reversible Rack (both layers)

**LEVEL 1 (BOTTOM OF POT)**

| | |
|---|---|
| 1 (14-ounce) box dry yellow rice | 3 cups water |

**LEVEL 2 (BOTTOM LAYER OF RACK)**
4 ears corn, shucked

**LEVEL 3 (TOP LAYER OF RACK)**

| | |
|---|---|
| 2 tablespoons canola oil, divided | Freshly ground black pepper |
| 1 tablespoon freshly squeezed lemon juice | 2 tablespoons prepared barbecue sauce |
| 2 tablespoons steak seasoning | 1 tablespoon Worcestershire sauce |
| 2 tablespoons kosher salt | 1 pound steak tips |

1. Start with the Level 3 ingredients: In a large resealable plastic bag, combine the oil, lemon juice, steak seasoning, salt, some pepper, the barbecue sauce, and Worcestershire sauce. Seal the bag and shake to mix the marinade well. Add the steak to the bag, reseal, and massage the outside of the bag to work the marinade over all parts of the steak. Place the bag in the refrigerator to marinate for at least 6 hours and up to 24 hours.

2. After the steak has marinated, put the rice and water (Level 1 ingredients) in the pot.

**3.** Place the bottom layer of the Deluxe Reversible Rack in the lower position, then place the rack in the pot. Place the corn on the rack.

**4.** Slide the Deluxe Layer through the lower layer's handles. Remove the steak tips from the marinade (discarding any excess marinade) and place in a single layer on the Deluxe Layer. It's okay if the pieces overlap, because they will decrease in size as they cook.

**5.** Close the lid and move the slider to STEAMCRISP. Select STEAM & CRISP, set the temperature to 400°F, and set the time to 5 minutes. Press START/STOP to begin cooking (PrE will display for about 18 minutes as the unit steams, then the timer will start counting down).

**6.** When cooking is complete, carefully remove the rack layers and stir the rice. Serve the rice warm with the steak and corn.

*Per serving:* *Calories: 782; Total Fat: 22g; Saturated Fat: 6g; Cholesterol: 82mg; Sodium: 648mg; Carbohydrates: 112g; Fiber: 6g; Protein: 35g*

# Beef Wellington

**SERVES 4**

*This is a simplified version of an all-time childhood favorite. My dad was the executive chef at the Hanover Inn at Dartmouth College for 22 years and is one of the most talented people I know. He has always been so generous with his craft—he hosted my sixth-grade class at the restaurant for cooking classes; taught me the intricacies of properly cooked eggs; showed my sister, my friends, and me how to clean and prepare our catch of the day while on vacation; and woke up early on Sundays to cook me and my pals brunch. The only drawback was the holidays. Every year my dad had to work on Christmas, so my mom, sister, and I would get dressed up and go to the restaurant to eat beef Wellington. I can still picture him coming out of the kitchen in his chef whites and the quintessential hat for a quick visit. It always made me feel so special, so this recipe is for him.* —by Kelly Gray

**NUT-FREE**

**Prep Time:** 30 minutes
**Total Cook Time:** 1 hour
**Sear/Sauté:** about
20 minutes
**Steam:** about 15 minutes
**Cook:** 25 minutes

**Accessories:** Cook &
Crisp™ Basket, blender or
food processor

1 (2½-pound/8-inch-long) beef tenderloin

2 tablespoons canola oil

Kosher salt

Freshly ground black pepper

1 (8-ounce) package button mushrooms, quartered

1 large shallot, quartered

2 garlic cloves, peeled

Leaves from 3 thyme sprigs

1 (8-ounce) package dried porcini mushrooms, finely chopped

2 tablespoons Dijon mustard

1 sheet frozen puff pastry, thawed

All-purpose flour, for dusting

½ cup water, for steaming

1. Move the slider to AIR FRY/STOVETOP. Select SEAR/SAUTÉ and set the temperature to HI-5. Select START/STOP to preheat the unit for 5 minutes.

2. While the unit is preheating, coat the beef with the oil and season with salt and pepper.

**3.** When the unit has preheated, place the meat in the pot and sear each side until deeply browned on all sides, about 10 minutes total. Remove the beef from the pot and set aside to cool. Leave any browned bits and rendered beef fat in the pot.

**4.** While the tenderloin is cooking, put the button mushrooms, shallot, and garlic in a food processor. Pulse the mixture about 10 times or until finely chopped.

**5.** Turn the SEAR/SAUTÉ temperature down to 3. Add the mushroom mixture and thyme to the pot with the beef fat and cook, stirring occasionally, for about 10 minutes or until the mixture is golden brown and most of the moisture has evaporated. Press START/STOP to stop cooking.

**6.** Transfer the mushroom mixture to a medium bowl and stir in the porcinis and mustard. Set the mixture aside to cool for about 5 minutes. Rinse the pot.

**7.** Dust a clean, dry work surface with flour. Place the puff pastry dough on the surface and lightly dust it and a rolling pin with flour. Firmly roll the pastry 3 times, always rolling it away from you. Turn the dough a quarter turn. Dust again with flour as necessary and continue rolling out and turning the pastry until it is 1/16 inch thick, or about half its original thickness.

**8.** Lightly oil a cutting board or work surface. Place the prepared pastry on the board. Spread the cooled mushroom mixture evenly on the pastry, leaving a clear 1-inch border around the perimeter.

**Hack It:** If you prefer your beef medium, set the time for 30 minutes.

CONTINUED >

**9.** Lay the beef on the mushrooms and roll the pastry up and around the beef, pressing to seal the ends and the edge where the puff pastry meets itself.

**10.** Place a 3½-by-8-inch piece of parchment in the Cook & Crisp™ Basket and place the beef, seam-side down, on top of the parchment.

**11.** Pour the water into the pot and place the Cook & Crisp™ Basket on top of the water.

**12.** Close the lid and move the slider to STEAMCRISP. Select STEAM & CRISP, set the temperature to 325ºF, and set the time to 25 minutes for medium-rare. Press START/STOP to begin cooking (PrE will display for about 15 minutes as the unit steams, then the timer will start counting down).

**13.** When cooking is complete, carefully remove the basket with the Wellington. Allow it to rest for 5 to 10 minutes, then slice and serve warm.

**Per serving:** *Calories: 1,261; Total Fat: 80g; Saturated Fat: 26g; Cholesterol: 241mg; Sodium: 418mg; Carbohydrates: 72g; Fiber: 8g; Protein: 68g*

# Brisket and Root Vegetables

**SERVES 4**

*Brisket with root vegetables is one of my go-to comfort food meals whenever I want something that is super rich and hearty. All you really need to do for this recipe is prep the ingredients and then let the Ninja® Foodi® SmartLid™ do all the work for you. The brisket comes out unbelievably tender from pressure cooking, and by air frying at the end of cooking, the vegetables achieve a nice roasted texture on the outside, making for a truly delicious meal.* —by Caroline Schliep

DAIRY-FREE
GLUTEN-FREE
NUT-FREE
STEAMCRISP MEALS

**Prep Time:** 5 minutes
**Total Cook Time:** 1 hour 50 minutes
**Sear/Sauté:** 15 minutes
**Pressure Build:** about 10 minutes
**Pressure Cook:** 55 minutes
**Pressure Release:** 30 minutes
**Air fry:** 10 minutes

**Accessories:** Deluxe Reversible Rack (bottom layer only)

**Substitution Tip:** If beef brisket isn't readily available in your grocery store, you could replace it with a 3-pound chuck roast.

**LEVEL 1 (BOTTOM OF POT)**

2 tablespoons canola oil

3 pounds beef brisket

Kosher salt

Freshly ground black pepper

½ cup red wine

1 white onion, diced

1 tablespoon minced garlic

1 tablespoon tomato paste

2 cups beef stock

3 tablespoons cornstarch

3 tablespoons water

**LEVEL 2 (TOP LAYER OF RACK)**

1 tablespoon canola oil

3 carrots, ends trimmed, quartered

1 pound baby Yukon Gold potatoes

Kosher salt

Freshly ground black pepper

**1.** Close the lid and move the slider to AIR FRY/STOVETOP. Select SEAR/SAUTÉ and set the temperature to HI-5. Open the lid and press START/STOP to begin preheating. Allow the unit to preheat for 5 minutes.

**2.** When the unit has preheated, prepare the Level 1 ingredients. Pour the oil into the pot. Season the brisket generously on both sides with salt and pepper. When the oil is hot, put the brisket in the pot and sear it for 5 minutes on each side or until browned. Remove the brisket from the pot and set aside.

**3.** Put the wine, onion, garlic, and tomato paste in the pot. Gently scrape up any browned bits from the bottom of the pot and cook, stirring frequently, until the onion is tender, about 5 minutes. Add the beef stock to the pot followed by the brisket. Press START/STOP to stop the cooking.

**4.** Combine the oil, carrots, and potatoes (Level 2 ingredients) in a large bowl. Season with salt and pepper and toss.

**5.** Place the bottom layer of the Deluxe Reversible Rack in the higher position, then cover it with a sheet of aluminum foil. Place the rack in the pot above the brisket. Place the carrots and potatoes on the foil.

**6.** Close the lid and move the slider to PRESSURE. Make sure the pressure release valve is in the SEAL position. The temperature will default to HIGH, which is the correct setting. Set the time to 55 minutes (the unit will build pressure for about 10 minutes before cooking begins).

**7.** When cooking is complete, select KEEP WARM, then naturally release the pressure for 30 minutes. Quick release the remaining pressure by turning the pressure release valve to the VENT position.

**8.** When all the pressure is released, move the slider to AIR FRY/STOVETOP. Select AIR FRY, set the temperature to 400°F, and set the time to 10 minutes. Select START/STOP to begin cooking.

**9.** When cooking is complete, remove the rack with the vegetables. Remove the brisket, place it in a baking dish or on a cutting board, and pull it apart with forks.

**10.** In a small bowl, whisk the cornstarch and water. Add this slurry to the liquid in the pot and stir until thickened, about 1 minute. Return the brisket to the pot, toss with the sauce, and serve with the vegetables.

**Per serving:** *Calories: 1,203; Total Fat: 86g; Saturated Fat: 31g; Cholesterol: 320mg; Sodium: 319mg; Carbohydrates: 34g; Fiber: 5g; Protein: 64g*

*CONTINUED >*

# Carne Asada Tacos

**SERVES 4**

*Taco night is always a favorite, and with the SmartLid™, taco night will be your favorite night as well. The key to this dish is marinating the meat for at least 6 hours, which will give you a very tender steak.* —by Myles Bryan

DAIRY-FREE
NUT-FREE

**Prep Time:** 15 minutes, plus 6 hours to marinate
**Total Cook Time:** 31 minutes
**Sear/Sauté:** 16 minutes
**Steam:** about 15 minutes

**Accessories:** Deluxe Reversible Rack (bottom layer)

*Per serving: Calories: 1,225; Total Fat: 40g; Saturated Fat: 14g; Cholesterol: 243mg; Sodium: 1636mg; Carbohydrates: 110g; Fiber: 3g; Protein: 98g*

## LEVEL 1 (BOTTOM OF POT)

- 4 slices uncooked bacon, diced
- 1 small yellow onion, peeled, diced
- 1 jalapeño, stemmed, seeded, diced
- 1 (12-ounce) bottle light beer
- 3 (15-ounce) cans pinto beans, rinsed and drained
- 1 teaspoon chili powder
- 1 teaspoon freshly squeezed lime juice
- 1 tablespoon brown sugar
- Kosher salt
- Freshly ground black pepper

## LEVEL 2 (TOP LAYER OF RACK)

- 3 (about 1 pound, ½- to 1-inch-thick) skirt steaks, cut into 8-inch-long strips
- 1 tablespoon minced garlic
- 1 tablespoon chopped fresh cilantro leaves
- 2 tablespoons Worcestershire sauce
- 1 tablespoon ground cumin
- 1½ cups pineapple juice
- 3 tablespoons freshly squeezed lime juice
- Kosher salt
- Freshly ground black pepper

## TOPPINGS (OPTIONAL)

- 8 flour tortillas
- Salsa
- Avocado
- Sour cream
- Lime wedges

**1.** Combine the steak, garlic, cilantro, Worcestershire sauce, cumin, pineapple juice and lime juice in a large resealable plastic bag. Season with salt and pepper. Massage the outside of the bag to work the marinade over the steak, then place the bag in the refrigerator to marinate for at least 6 hours and up to 24 hours.

*CONTINUED >*

**2.** After the steak has marinated, prepare the Level 1 ingredients: Close the lid and move the slider to AIR FRY/ STOVETOP. Select SEAR/SAUTÉ and set the temperature to HI-5. Open the lid and select START/STOP to begin preheating. Allow the unit to preheat for 5 minutes.

**3.** Once the unit has preheated, add the bacon and cook, stirring occasionally, until golden brown, 5 to 10 minutes. Using a slotted spoon, transfer the bacon to a paper towel–lined plate and set aside.

**4.** Place the onion and jalapeño in the pot and cook in the rendered bacon fat until the onion is translucent, about 5 minutes. Add the beer, pinto beans, chili powder, lime juice, and brown sugar to the pot. Season with salt and pepper and stir until fully combined.

**5.** Remove the steak pieces from the marinade (discard any excess marinade) and place them on the bottom layer of the Deluxe Reversible Rack in the higher position, then place the rack in the pot over the beans and vegetables. It's okay if the pieces overlap, because they will decrease in size as they cook.

**6.** Close the lid and move the slider to STEAMCRISP. Select STEAM & CRISP, set the temperature to 400°F, and set the time to 6 minutes. Press START/STOP to begin cooking (PrE will display for about 15 minutes as the unit steams, then the timer will start counting down).

**7.** When cooking is complete, carefully remove the rack with the steak. Let the steak rest for 5 minutes. Stir the beans and leave them in the pot uncovered while the steak rests. Thinly slice the steak. Assemble the tacos with steak, beans, the reserved bacon, and toppings of your choice. Serve hot.

# Lamb Roast with Rosemary Potatoes

**SERVES 4 TO 6**

*This recipe is a nod to the many years of family holiday gatherings with a roast. My dad would make many variations on lamb, along with potatoes and another side dish. It was a long, time-consuming effort to do in the oven, and I remember him having to get up early to ensure we would eat on time. With this recipe, you won't be waiting on the oven in order to get a great holiday meal on the table for your entire family.* —by Meg Jordan

**DAIRY-FREE**
**NUT-FREE**

**Prep Time:** 10 minutes
**Total Cook Time:** about 45 minutes
**Steam:** about 15 minutes
**Cook:** 25 to 35 minutes (depending on desired doneness)

**Accessories:** Deluxe Reversible Rack (bottom layer only)

**LEVEL 1 (BOTTOM OF POT)**
5 cups beef stock
4 garlic cloves, peeled
1 tablespoon whole black peppercorns
3 tablespoons instant flour

**LEVEL 2 (BOTTOM LAYER OF RACK)**
3 cups baby potatoes, halved
2 rosemary sprigs, minced
2 tablespoons canola oil, divided
Kosher salt
Freshly ground black pepper
2 pounds boneless lamb loin

1. Start with the Level 1 ingredients: Put the beef stock, garlic, and peppercorns in the pot and stir until combined.

2. Prepare the Level 2 ingredients: In a large bowl, combine the potatoes, rosemary, and 1 tablespoon of oil. Season with salt and pepper and toss until evenly combined.

3. Rub the remaining 1 tablespoon of oil on the lamb and season generously with salt and pepper.

4. Place the bottom layer of the Deluxe Reversible Rack in the lower position, then place the rack in the pot above the gravy mixture. Add three-quarters of the potatoes to the rack, then place the lamb on top of the potatoes. Top the meat with the remaining potatoes.

*CONTINUED >*

**5.** Close the lid and move the slider to STEAMCRISP. Select STEAM & CRISP, set the temperature to 360°F, and set the time for 25 minutes. Press START/STOP to begin cooking (PrE will display for about 15 minutes as the unit steams, then the timer will start counting down).

**6.** After 25 minutes, check the roast with an instant-read thermometer. For medium-rare it should read 145°F. If you prefer the roast cooked medium to medium well, continue cooking for up to 10 minutes more.

**7.** When cooking is complete, carefully remove the rack with the potatoes and the roast. Allow the roast to rest for 10 minutes.

**8.** While the roast is resting, use a silicone or wooden spoon to stir in the instant flour until the sauce has thickened. If a thicker sauce is desired, move the slider to the right position, select SEAR/SAUTÉ, and set the temperature to 3. Continue to cook until the sauce reaches your desired thickness.

**9.** Strain the gravy through a fine-mesh strainer. Slice the roast and serve with the potatoes and gravy.

*Per serving: Calories: 635; Total Fat: 37g; Saturated Fat: 15g; Cholesterol: 150mg; Sodium: 205mg; Carbohydrates: 25g; Fiber: 3g; Protein: 47g*

**Key Lime Cheesecake with Mango Sauce,** *page 192*

# 9

# Desserts, Breads, and Rolls

# Key Lime Cheesecake with Mango Sauce

**SERVES 8**

*This was by far the most delicious recipe to develop, and we all welcomed the many mistakes in trying to nail down the perfect flavor. It's hard to go wrong with a cheesecake in the Ninja® Foodi® SmartLid™. The Steam & Bake function makes the tenderest, softest baked goods—a winner all around! If you don't love mango, substitute any frozen fruit for the sauce.* —by Kara Bleday

NUT-FREE
VEGETARIAN

**Prep Time:** 20 minutes
**Total Cook Time:**
45 minutes
**Steam:** about 20 minutes
**Bake:** 25 minutes

**Accessories:** Ninja®
Multi-Purpose Pan or
8-inch round baking pan,
Deluxe Reversible Rack
(bottom layer only)

**FOR THE CRUST**
1¼ cups graham
   cracker crumbs

2 tablespoons
   granulated sugar

6 tablespoons (¾ stick)
   unsalted butter, melted

⅛ teaspoon kosher salt

**FOR THE FILLING**
2 (8-ounce) packages
   (2 cups) cream cheese,
   at room temperature

⅔ cup granulated sugar

¼ cup key lime juice

3 tablespoons sour cream,
   at room temperature

1 teaspoon pure
   vanilla extract

1 teaspoon grated lime zest

2 large eggs, at room
   temperature

**FOR THE MANGO SAUCE**
3 cups frozen
   mango chunks

¾ cup water

¼ cup granulated sugar

1 teaspoon freshly
   squeezed lemon juice

1. **To make the crust:** Combine the graham cracker crumbs, sugar, butter, and salt in a large bowl and mix thoroughly. Transfer the mixture to the Multi-Purpose Pan and press into an even layer across the bottom and up the sides of the pan. Make the crust on the bottom thicker than on the sides.

**2. To make the filling:** In a large bowl, beat the cream cheese and sugar together until smooth. If using a hand or stand mixer, use medium speed. Add the key lime juice, sour cream, vanilla, lime zest, and eggs and continue to beat until fully combined. Pour the filling into the crust.

**3. To make the mango sauce:** Put the mango sauce ingredients in the pot and stir until evenly combined.

**4.** Place the pan on the bottom layer of the Deluxe Reversible Rack in the lower position, then place the rack in the pot.

**5.** Close the lid and move the slider to STEAMCRISP. Select STEAM & BAKE, set the temperature to 250°F, and set the time to 25 minutes. Select START/STOP to begin cooking (PrE will display for about 20 minutes as the unit steams, then the timer will start counting down).

**6.** When cooking is complete, the cheesecake will still be jiggly in the center. Remove the rack and pan and allow to cool for about 30 minutes. Refrigerate the cheesecake for at least 1 hour before serving to give it a firmer texture.

**7.** While the cheesecake is cooling, mash the mangos with a fork or blend them quickly in a blender to make a smoother sauce. Combine the mashed mango with the water, sugar, and lemon juice.

**8.** Take the cheesecake out the refrigerator, slice with a wet knife, and serve with the mango sauce. The cheesecake will last up to 5 days, covered, in the refrigerator.

**Hack It:** If you can't find graham cracker crumbs in the grocery store, put 10 whole crackers into a quart-size bag, seal the bag, and use a rolling pin to crush the crackers.

*Per serving: Calories: 495; Total Fat: 32g; Saturated Fat: 17g; Cholesterol: 134mg; Sodium: 328mg; Carbohydrates: 49g; Fiber: 2g; Protein: 7g*

# Orange Upside-Down Olive Oil Cake

**SERVES 8 TO 12**

*This orange upside-down cake is a citrusy spin on your classic pineapple upside-down cake. It may sound complicated, but in reality, the cake is super simple to make. The oranges soak up all the delicious caramel made from the butter and sugar in the bottom of the pan. This almost candies the oranges, which pairs nicely with the light and airy cake. Dust this thing with some powdered sugar and—voilà!—a showstopper for your next gathering.* —by Caroline Schliep

**NUT-FREE**
**VEGETARIAN**

**Prep Time:** 5 minutes
**Total Cook Time:**
45 minutes
**Steam:** about 20 minutes
**Bake:** 25 minutes

**Accessories:** Ninja®
Multi-Purpose Pan or
8-inch round baking pan,
Deluxe Reversible Rack
(bottom layer only)

- 3 cups water, for steaming
- Nonstick cooking spray
- 3 tablespoons unsalted butter, melted
- 3 tablespoons brown sugar
- 1 navel orange, stem and bottom ends trimmed, cut into ¼-inch rounds
- ¾ cup granulated sugar
- ½ cup vanilla Greek yogurt
- ¼ cup freshly squeezed orange juice
- 2 tablespoons grated orange zest
- ½ cup extra-virgin olive oil
- 3 large eggs
- 1½ cups all-purpose flour
- 1½ teaspoons baking powder
- ⅛ teaspoon kosher salt
- ¼ cup powdered sugar, for dusting

**1.** Pour the water into the pot. Spray the Multi-Purpose Pan with cooking spray and set aside.

**2.** In a small bowl, whisk the butter and brown sugar together until the sugar has dissolved. Spread the sugar mixture evenly across the bottom of the prepared pan. Arrange the orange slices over the brown sugar mixture in a single layer. Set aside.

**3.** In a large bowl, combine the granulated sugar, yogurt, orange juice, orange zest, olive oil, and eggs and mix thoroughly. Add the flour, baking powder, and salt and continue to mix until combined. Pour the batter evenly over the orange slices.

**4.** Place the pan on the bottom layer of the Deluxe Reversible Rack in the lower position, then place the rack in the pot.

**5.** Close the lid and move the slider to STEAMCRISP. Select STEAM & BAKE, set the temperature to 285°F, and set the time to 25 minutes. Press START/STOP to begin cooking (PrE will display for about 20 minutes as the unit steams, then the timer will start counting down).

**6.** When cooking is complete, check for doneness by inserting a wooden toothpick into the middle of the cake. If it comes out clean, remove the rack with the pan and let it cool for at least 1 hour. If the toothpick comes out with moist crumbs stuck to it, bake for 5 more minutes or until the toothpick comes out clean.

**7.** When the cake has cooled, place a cake plate over the top of the cake and invert the plate and pan to flip the cake onto the plate. Dust with powdered sugar and serve.

**Per serving:** *Calories: 390; Total Fat: 20g; Saturated Fat: 6g; Cholesterol: 83mg; Sodium: 76mg; Carbohydrates: 47g; Fiber: 1g; Protein: 6g*

**Variation Tip:** You can replace the oranges in this recipe with any fruit of your choice, creating a different spin on this cake. Try thinly sliced pineapple (classic!), apple, peach, pear, or plum.

# Two-Layer Chocolate Strawberry Birthday Cake

**SERVES 8 TO 10**

*"Birthday cake" can be an intimidating pair of words: The pressure to create a showstopper feels baked into them. However, that doesn't have to be the case. With this recipe, you simply tinker with store-bought chocolate cake mix to create a taller-than-average cake that you cut in half across the middle rather than having to bake two separate layers. While the cake bakes, stir together an easy strawberry buttercream to tie this decadent summery treat together.*
—by Avery Lowe

**NUT-FREE**

**Prep Time:** 10 minutes
**Total Cook Time:**
45 minutes
**Steam:** about 20 minutes
**Bake:** 25 minutes

**Accessories:** Ninja®
Multi-Purpose Pan or
8-inch round baking pan,
Deluxe Reversible Rack
(bottom layer only)

3¾ cups water, divided

Nonstick cooking spray

4 tablespoons all-purpose
flour, divided

1 (16-ounce) box
chocolate cake mix

2 large eggs plus
2 egg whites

½ cup canola oil or
vegetable oil

3 sticks (1½ cups)
unsalted butter, at
room temperature

4 cups powdered sugar

1 teaspoon pure
vanilla extract

2 cups very ripe
strawberries, stemmed
and smashed with a fork

1. Pour 3 cups of water into the pot. Spray the bottom of the Multi-Purpose Pan with cooking spray and dust with 2 tablespoons of flour.

2. Combine the cake mix and the remaining 2 tablespoons of flour in a large bowl and mix thoroughly. In a separate large bowl, stir together the eggs and egg whites, the remaining ¾ cup of water, and the oil until combined.

3. Slowly add the dry ingredients to the wet and stir just until combined. Pour the batter into the prepared pan.

4. Place the pan on the bottom layer of the Deluxe Reversible Rack in the lower position, then place the rack in the pot.

*CONTINUED >*

**Substitution Tip:** Don't have fresh strawberries? Frozen work, too. Just microwave for 30 seconds and then mash with a fork.

**5.** Close the lid and move the slider to STEAMCRISP. Select STEAM & BAKE, set the temperature to 285ºF, and set the time to 25 minutes. Press START/STOP to begin cooking (PrE will display for about 20 minutes as the unit steams, then the timer will start counting down).

**6.** While the cake is baking, prepare the frosting. Put the butter in a large bowl. Using a hand or stand mixer on medium speed, cream the butter on high speed for 30 seconds. Gradually add the powdered sugar and vanilla. Once the frosting has come together, beat in the strawberries.

**7.** When cooking is complete, check for doneness by inserting a wooden toothpick into the middle of the cake. If it comes out clean, remove the rack with the pan. If the toothpick comes out with moist crumbs stuck to it, bake for 5 more minutes or until the toothpick comes out clean.

**8.** Remove the pan from the pot. Rest the pan on the counter and let cool for at least 1 hour.

**9.** Once the cake has cooled, flip the cake onto a plate, and use a serrated knife to slice it in half horizontally to create two layers. Place the bottom cake layer on a plate, cut-side up, and evenly cover with half the frosting. Place the second layer on top of the first, cut-side down, and frost the top and sides of the cake. Serve and enjoy.

*Per serving: Calories: 875; Total Fat: 51g; Saturated Fat: 25g; Cholesterol: 138mg; Sodium: 515mg; Carbohydrates: 103g; Fiber: 3g; Protein: 6g*

# Chocolate Chip Zucchini Bread

**SERVES 6 TO 8**

*Zucchini bread is a delicious and moist breakfast or dessert that is truly trans-formed by the Ninja® Foodi® SmartLid™. The addition of chocolate chips makes for an extra special sweet treat. By using box cake mix, this batter can be made in minutes and the bread ready within the hour.* —by Michelle Boland

**NUT-FREE**
**VEGETARIAN**

**Prep Time:** 10 minutes
**Total Cook Time:**
45 minutes
**Steam:** about 20 minutes
**Bake:** 25 minutes

**Accessories:** Ninja®
Multi-Purpose Pan or
8-inch-round baking pan,
Deluxe Reversible Rack
(bottom layer only)

1½ cups water, for steaming
Nonstick cooking spray
1 (16-ounce) box
  yellow cake mix
1 teaspoon ground
  cinnamon
½ cup canola or
  vegetable oil

¼ cup whole milk
3 large eggs
2 cups coarsely
  shredded zucchini
½ cup chocolate chips

1. Pour the water into the pot. Spray the Multi-Purpose Pan with cooking spray.

2. In a large bowl, whisk together the cake mix, cinnamon, oil, milk, and eggs until smooth and combined.

3. Fold the zucchini and chocolate chips into the batter. Pour the batter into the prepared pan.

4. Place the pan on the bottom layer of the Deluxe reversible Rack in the lower position, then place the rack in the pot.

5. Close the lid and move the slider to STEAMCRISP. Select STEAM & BAKE, set the temperature to 285ºF, and set the time to 25 minutes. Press START/STOP to begin cooking (PrE will display for about 20 minutes as the unit steams, then the timer will start counting down).

*CONTINUED >*

**6.** When cooking is complete, check for doneness by inserting a wooden toothpick into the middle of the cake. If it comes out clean, remove the rack with the pan and let it cool for at least 1 hour. If the toothpick comes out with moist crumbs stuck to it, bake for 5 more minutes or until the toothpick comes out clean.

*Per serving: Calories: 603; Total Fat: 33g; Saturated Fat: 7g; Cholesterol: 95mg; Sodium: 694mg; Carbohydrates: 69g; Fiber: 2g; Protein: 8g*

# Garlic Dinner Rolls

**MAKES 12 ROLLS**

*When I was growing up, my favorite part of going out to dinner was always the breadbasket. Arriving at the restaurant hungry and immediately eating a buttery roll always sat well with me. With this recipe, you can make your own restaurant-worthy bread by proofing the rolls in the SmartLid™, where the preset temperature settings and controlled environment will help these rolls rise consistently every time. And once the rise times are complete, these rolls bake in only 10 minutes. Mix up the buttery topping with whatever goes best with what you're serving that day.* —by Avery Lowe

**NUT-FREE**
**VEGETARIAN**

**Prep Time:** 10 minutes
**Proof:** 45 minutes
(first rise) + 25 minutes
(second rise)
**Total Cook Time:**
15 minutes
**Steam:** about 5 minutes
**Bake:** 10 minutes

**Accessories:** Ninja®
Multi-Purpose Pan or
8-inch-round baking pan,
Deluxe Reversible Rack
(bottom layer only)

- 8 tablespoons (1 stick) unsalted butter, divided (7 tablespoons melted, 1 tablespoon at room temperature)
- 1 (0.25 ounce) package active dry yeast
- ¾ cup warm water, divided
- ¾ cup whole milk, warmed
- ¼ cup granulated sugar
- 2 large eggs, beaten
- ½ teaspoon kosher salt
- 3 cups all-purpose flour, plus more as needed and more for dusting
- 1 tablespoon garlic powder
- 1 tablespoon fresh rosemary, minced

**1.** Coat the Multi-Purpose Pan with 1 tablespoon of room-temperature butter.

**2.** In a small bowl, whisk together the yeast and ¼ cup of warm water until combined. Let sit until foamy, about 5 minutes. In a separate small bowl, whisk together the milk, 4 tablespoons of melted butter, and the sugar. Set aside until cooled, about 5 minutes.

**3.** Transfer the yeast mixture and milk mixture to a large bowl and whisk until combined. Add the eggs, salt, and ½ cup of flour at a time until the dough comes together.

CONTINUED >

**4.** Dust a clean work surface with flour. Place the dough on the surface and knead it into a smooth ball, about 5 minutes. If the dough is sticky, add additional flour 1 tablespoon at a time to prevent sticking.

**5.** Place the dough ball in the prepared pan. Place the pan on the bottom layer of the Deluxe Reversible Rack in the lower position, then place the rack in the pot.

**6.** Close the lid and move the slider to AIR FRY/ STOVETOP. Select PROOF, set the temperature to 80°F, and set the time to 45 minutes. Press START/STOP to begin the first rise.

**7.** When the first rise is complete, remove the dough from the pan and place it on the floured work surface. Punch down the dough gently by pressing into it, then divide it into 12 equal pieces. Shape each piece into a small ball and place each in the pan. The rolls should be touching but with visible gaps between them.

**8.** Pour the remaining ½ cup of water into the pot. Place the pan back on the rack in the pot.

**9.** Close the lid. Select PROOF, set the temperature to 80°F, and set the time to 25 minutes. Press START/STOP to begin the second rise.

**10.** When the second rise is complete, move the slider to STEAMCRISP. Select STEAM & BAKE, set the temperature to 300°F, and set the time to 10 minutes. Select START/STOP to begin (PrE will display for about 5 minutes as the unit steams, then the timer will start counting down).

**11.** While the rolls are baking, prepare the garlic rosemary butter. In a small bowl, whisk together the remaining 3 tablespoons of melted butter, the garlic powder, and rosemary until combined.

**12.** When cooking is complete, remove the pan from the pot and brush the rolls with the butter. Allow the rolls to cool for 15 minutes before serving.

*Per serving: Calories: 224; Total Fat: 9g; Saturated Fat: 5g; Cholesterol: 53mg; Sodium: 69mg; Carbohydrates: 30g; Fiber: 1g; Protein: 5g*

**Variation Tip:** Any herb, fresh or dried, can be subbed in for the fresh rosemary. Thyme or oregano work well.

# Sourdough Bread

**MAKES 1 LOAF**

*Sourdough bread is made traditionally with a starter that is a fermented mix of flour and water. Starters need to be "fed" often to be ready when you want to make bread. I've simplified this sourdough bread recipe by using sour cream and Greek yogurt in place of the traditional starter. That means you can now make sourdough bread in less than a day, and you don't have to feed a starter. And to top it off, the Ninja® Foodi® SmartLid™ also has a proofing function, making this recipe perfect for the home cook who wants bakery-quality results.* —by Caroline Schliep

**NUT-FREE**
**VEGETARIAN**

**Prep Time:** 15 minutes
**Proof:** 30 minutes
(first rise) + 30 minutes
(second rise)
**Total Cook Time:** 1 hour
**Steam:** about 5 minutes
**Bake:** 55 minutes

**Accessories:** Cook & Crisp™ Basket

¼ **cup water, for steaming**
**Nonstick cooking spray**
3 **cups bread flour, plus**
  **additional for dusting**
2 **cups plain Greek yogurt**

½ **cup sour cream**
1 **teaspoon active dry yeast**
1 **teaspoon kosher salt**

1. Pour the water into the pot. Lay an 8-inch circle of parchment paper in the bottom of the Cook & Crisp™ Basket, spray the paper with cooking spray, and place the basket in the pot.

2. In a large bowl, mix together the flour, yogurt, sour cream, yeast, and salt until a dough ball forms.

3. Dust a clean work surface with flour and place the dough ball on it. Knead the dough until it is no longer sticky, 7 to 10 minutes. Form the dough into a ball, then place it seam-side down in the prepared basket.

4. Close the lid and move the slider to AIR FRY/ STOVETOP. Select PROOF, set the temperature to 95°F, and set the time to 30 minutes. Press START/STOP to begin the first rise.

**5.** When the rise is complete, remove the basket from the pot and turn the dough out onto the floured surface. Knead gently for 3 minutes, then form it into a ball again.

**6.** Return the basket to the pot and place the dough ball seam-side down on top of the parchment paper.

**7.** Close the lid and move the slider to AIR FRY/ STOVETOP. Select PROOF, set the temperature to 95°F, and set the time to 30 minutes. Press START/STOP to begin the second rise.

**8.** Once the second rise is complete, move the slider to STEAMCRISP. Select STEAM & CRISP, set the temperature to 300°F, and set the time to 55 minutes. Press START/STOP to begin cooking (PrE will display for about 5 minutes as the unit steams, then the timer will start counting down).

**9.** When cooking is complete, the surface of the bread will be crusty and brown. Remove the bread from the basket and allow to cool completely before serving.

**Ingredient Info:** This sourdough bread tastes sour due to the lactic acid bacteria found in the yogurt and sour cream.

*Per serving (8 servings): Calories: 238; Total Fat: 5g; Saturated Fat: 3g; Cholesterol: 15mg; Sodium: 181mg; Carbohydrates: 39g; Fiber: 1g; Protein: 7g*

# Rosemary Bread

**MAKES 2 DOUGH BALLS**

*Bread making at home has become a huge trend, especially with many of us now at home more often. I've never been able to master bread baking in my wall oven; sometimes the bread is too dry or the texture is just not right. With the Steam & Crisp function on the Ninja® Foodi® SmartLid™, I'm able to get a great chewy interior and beautiful crusty exterior. By adding some herbs, I can make different varieties of bread and impress my breadmaking friends.* —by Meg Jordan

**NUT-FREE**
**VEGAN**

**Prep Time:** 15 minutes
**Proof:** 50 minutes
(first rise) + 50 minutes
(second rise)
**Total Cook Time:**
25 minutes
**Steam:** about 5 minutes
**Cook:** 20 minutes

**Accessories:** Cook &
Crisp™ Basket

- 4 cups all-purpose flour, divided, plus more for dusting
- 2½ teaspoons instant yeast
- 1¾ cups lukewarm water, divided
- 1½ teaspoons kosher salt
- 2½ tablespoons extra-virgin olive oil
- ¼ cup minced fresh rosemary leaves
- Nonstick cooking spray

1. In a stand mixer or large mixing bowl, combine 3½ cups of flour, the yeast, 1½ cups of lukewarm water, and the salt, olive oil, and rosemary. Mix until a smooth, sticky dough forms. If necessary, add the remaining flour ½ tablespoon at a time.

2. Dust a clean work surface with flour. Transfer the dough to the surface and knead by hand until the dough becomes smooth and forms a ball, about 5 minutes.

3. Cut the dough into 2 equal-size portions and form each into a ball. Reserve 1 dough ball for the recipe. Place the second ball in a sealed container with headspace and store in the refrigerator for up to 3 days.

4. Line the Cook & Crisp™ Basket with a nonstick silicone baking mat or parchment paper, and spray with cooking spray. Transfer the dough to the basket. Place the basket in the pot.

**5.** Close the lid, then move the slider to AIR FRY/STOVE TOP. Select PROOF, set the temperature to 95ºF, and the time to 50 minutes. Press START/STOP to begin the first rise.

**6.** When the rise is complete, remove the basket and place the dough on the floured work surface. Pour the remaining ¼ cup of water into the pot.

**7.** Deflate the dough by gently pressing on it, then reshape it into a ball. Place the dough back in the basket, then place the basket in the pot. Close the lid.

**8.** Select PROOF, set the temperature to 95ºF, and set the time to 50 minutes. Press START/STOP to begin the second rise. After 30 minutes check the dough to see if it has doubled in size. If it has not doubled in size, close the lid and continue proofing for the remaining 20 minutes.

**9.** Once the dough has doubled in size, close the lid and move the slider to STEAMCRISP. Select STEAM & CRISP, set the temperature to 350ºF, and set the time to 20 minutes. Select START/STOP to begin (PrE will display for about 5 minutes as the unit steams, then the time will start counting down).

**10.** When cooking is complete, the surface of the bread will be crusty and brown. Carefully remove the basket from the pot. Allow the bread to cool for at least 30 minutes before serving.

**Substitution Tip:** Customize by using different herbs, such as oregano or sage.

**Per serving (16 servings):** *Calories: 135; Total Fat: 3g; Saturated Fat: 0g; Cholesterol: 0mg; Sodium: 110mg; Carbohydrates: 24g; Fiber: 1g; Protein: 3g*

# Cheesy Bread Sticks

**SERVES 4**

*I have a problem: I am a carbivore. I knead bread! This recipe is cheesy, just like my puns, but it's also very easy because there isn't much prep. I love using store-bought pizza dough for things when I am feeling lazy, which is a lot when I'm at home. I love keeping a ball of pizza dough in the freezer just for occasions like this. Be sure to serve these bread sticks with your favorite pasta dishes from this book.*
—by Craig White

**NUT-FREE**

**Prep Time:** 10 minutes
**Total Cook Time:**
22 minutes
**Steam:** about 15 minutes
**Cook:** 7 minutes

**Accessories:** Deluxe Reversible Rack (bottom layer only), Ninja® Multi-Purpose Pan or 8-inch round baking pan

¾ cup water, for steaming

Nonstick cooking spray

1 (16-ounce) package store-bought pizza dough, at room temperature

2 tablespoons all-purpose flour, for dusting

½ cup shredded mozzarella cheese

2 teaspoons olive oil

½ teaspoon Italian seasoning

2 teaspoons grated Parmesan cheese

¼ teaspoon sea salt

**1.** Pour the water into the pot. Lightly spray the Multi-Purpose Pan with nonstick spray.

**2.** Portion the pizza dough into four (4-ounce) balls. Dust a work surface with the flour and roll each ball into an 8-inch-long rope. Then roll each rope into an 8-by-2-inch rectangle.

**3.** With a long end of one rectangle parallel to you, sprinkle the piece of dough with 2 tablespoons of mozzarella cheese. Fold the edge of the dough nearest you over the cheese and pinch to seal the edges. Roll the dough by hand again and reform into an 8-inch-long bread stick. Repeat with the remaining dough rectangles.

**4.** Place the bread sticks in the prepared pan, drizzle the bread sticks with the olive oil, and rub them to coat thoroughly. Sprinkle each with the Italian seasoning, Parmesan cheese, and sea salt.

**5.** Place the bottom layer of the Deluxe Reversible Rack in the lower position, place the pan onto the rack, then place the rack in the pot.

**6.** Close the lid and move the slider to STEAMCRISP. Select STEAM & BAKE, set the temperature to 325°F, and set the time to 7 minutes. Press START/STOP to begin cooking (PrE will display for about 15 minutes as the unit steams, then the timer will start counting down).

**7.** When cooking is complete, carefully remove the pan and serve the bread sticks warm.

**Per serving:** *Calories: 356; Total Fat: 9g; Saturated Fat: 3g; Cholesterol: 12mg; Sodium: 836mg; Carbohydrates: 56g; Fiber: 3g; Protein: 14g*

**Variation Tip:** Don't have dried herbs? Feel free to use fresh herbs such as rosemary or oregano.

# Chipotle-Cheddar Corn Bread

**SERVES 6 TO 8**

*Corn bread is a great appetizer or side, and it is fantastic when made in the SmartLid™. Combining steam with convection baking gives this corn bread an amazing rise and texture. The chipotle and cheddar put a fun spin on the usual, and this chipotle-cheddar corn bread couldn't be easier to make.*
—by Michelle Boland

NUT-FREE
VEGETARIAN

**Prep Time:** 5 minutes
**Total Cook Time:**
40 minutes
**Steam:** about 20 minutes
**Bake:** 20 minutes

**Accessories:** Ninja®
Multi-Purpose Pan or
8-inch-round baking pan,
Deluxe Reversible Rack
(bottom layer only)

*Per serving: Calories: 434;
Total Fat: 17g; Saturated Fat: 6g;
Cholesterol: 81mg; Sodium:
783mg; Carbohydrates: 57g;
Fiber: 5g; Protein: 12g*

**3 cups water, for steaming**

**Nonstick cooking spray**

**2 (8.5-ounce) boxes
corn bread mix**

**2 large eggs**

**⅔ cup whole milk**

**2 tablespoons ancho chili
paste or 2 tablespoons
adobo sauce from a
can of chipotle chiles**

**¾ cup shredded
cheddar cheese**

1. Pour the water into the pot. Spray the Multi-Purpose Pan with cooking spray.

2. In a large bowl, whisk together the corn bread mix, eggs, milk, chili paste, and cheddar cheese until combined and smooth. Pour the batter into the prepared pan.

3. Place the pan on the bottom layer of the Deluxe Reversible Rack in the lower position, then place the rack in the pot.

4. Close the lid and move the slider to STEAMCRISP. Select STEAM & BAKE, set the temperature to 385°F, and set the time to 20 minutes. Press START/STOP to begin cooking (PrE will display for about 20 minutes as the unit steams, then the timer will start counting down).

5. When cooking is complete, check for doneness by inserting a wooden toothpick into the middle of the corn bread. If it comes out clean, remove the rack with the pan and let cool for at least 1 hour. If the toothpick comes out with moist crumbs stuck to it, bake for 5 more minutes or until the toothpick comes out clean. Cool before serving.

# Tomato, Onion, and Pesto Focaccia

**SERVES 6 TO 8**

*One of the best features of the Foodi® SmartLid™ is the fact that you can make fresh bread in under an hour from start to finish—meaning you can have fresh baked bread on the table for dinner or as an anytime snack. The Proof function makes proofing super simple and keeps everything in one pot, ready for baking. Simply top the proofed dough with a variety of ingredients, steam and bake the bread, and the result is fresh, hot, and delicious.* —by Melissa Celli

**NUT-FREE**

**Prep Time:** 5 minutes
**Proof:** 30 minutes
**Total Cook Time:**
20 minutes
**Steam:** about 5 minutes
**Cook:** 15 minutes

**Accessories:** Cook & Crisp™ Basket

¼ **cup water, for steaming**

**Nonstick cooking spray**

1 **(16-ounce) package store-bought pizza dough, at room temperature**

1 **tablespoon extra-virgin olive oil**

1 **heaping tablespoon prepared pesto**

10 **cherry tomatoes, halved**

1 **small red onion, thinly sliced**

¼ **cup shredded Parmesan cheese**

1. Pour the water into the pot.

2. Lay an 8-inch circle of parchment paper in the bottom of the Cook & Crisp™ Basket and spray with cooking spray. Form the dough into a ball and place it in the basket. Place the basket in the pot.

3. Close the lid and move the slider to AIR FRY/ STOVETOP. Select PROOF, set the temperature to 95ºF, and set the time to 30 minutes. Press START/STOP to begin the rise.

4. When the rise is complete, remove the basket from the pot. Deflate the dough by gently pressing on it, then spread it with your fingertips into the bottom of the basket. Drizzle the dough with the olive oil, spread the pesto over the dough, and top with the tomatoes and onion.

*CONTINUED >*

## Tomato, Onion, and Pesto Focaccia continued

**Hack It:** If using frozen dough, allow the dough to thaw before proofing. If using dough right from the refrigerator, proof it for 1 hour at 95°F.

5. Return the basket to the pot. Close the lid and move the slider to STEAMCRISP. Select STEAM & CRISP, set the temperature to 335ºF, and set the time to 15 minutes. Press START/STOP to begin cooking (PrE will display for about 5 minutes as the unit steams, then the timer will start counting down).

6. With 2 minutes left on the timer, open the lid and top the bread with the Parmesan cheese. Close the lid to finish cooking.

7. When cooking is complete, the surface of the focaccia will be crusty and brown. Remove from the basket and allow to cool for 5 minutes before serving.

*Per serving: Calories: 246; Total Fat: 7g; Saturated Fat: 2g; Cholesterol: 4mg; Sodium: 536mg; Carbohydrates: 38g; Fiber: 3g; Protein: 8g*

# MEASUREMENT CONVERSIONS

### VOLUME EQUIVALENTS (LIQUID)

| US Standard | US Standard (ounces) | Metric (approximate) |
|---|---|---|
| 2 tablespoons | 1 fl. oz. | 30 mL |
| ¼ cup | 2 fl. oz. | 60 mL |
| ½ cup | 4 fl. oz. | 120 mL |
| 1 cup | 8 fl. oz. | 240 mL |
| 1½ cups | 12 fl. oz. | 355 mL |
| 2 cups or 1 pint | 16 fl. oz. | 475 mL |
| 4 cups or 1 quart | 32 fl. oz. | 1 L |
| 1 gallon | 128 fl. oz. | 4 L |

### OVEN TEMPERATURES

| Fahrenheit (F) | Celsius (C) (approximate) |
|---|---|
| 250°F | 120°C |
| 300°F | 150°C |
| 325°F | 165°C |
| 350°F | 180°C |
| 375°F | 190°C |
| 400°F | 200°C |
| 425°F | 220°C |
| 450°F | 230°C |

### VOLUME EQUIVALENTS (DRY)

| US Standard | Metric (approximate) |
|---|---|
| ⅛ teaspoon | 0.5 mL |
| ¼ teaspoon | 1 mL |
| ½ teaspoon | 2 mL |
| ¾ teaspoon | 4 mL |
| 1 teaspoon | 5 mL |
| 1 tablespoon | 15 mL |
| ¼ cup | 59 mL |
| ⅓ cup | 79 mL |
| ½ cup | 118 mL |
| ⅔ cup | 156 mL |
| ¾ cup | 177 mL |
| 1 cup | 235 mL |
| 2 cups or 1 pint | 475 mL |
| 3 cups | 700 mL |
| 4 cups or 1 quart | 1 L |

### WEIGHT EQUIVALENTS

| US Standard | Metric (approximate) |
|---|---|
| ½ ounce | 15 g |
| 1 ounce | 30 g |
| 2 ounces | 60 g |
| 4 ounces | 115 g |
| 8 ounces | 225 g |
| 12 ounces | 340 g |
| 16 ounces or 1 pound | 455 g |

# COOKING TIME CHARTS

## Steam & Crisp Chart

Steaming & Crisping is a great way to get food that has a crispy exterior but is juicy inside. Before placing the food and accessory into the unit, ensure that you've added water to the bottom of the cooking pot. This is important to ensure that steam will be produced and get you those delicious results you desire.

| INGREDIENT | AMOUNT | PREPARATION | OIL *optional* | WATER |
|---|---|---|---|---|
| **VEGETABLES** | | | | |
| Acorn squash | 1 | Cut in half, placed face down | 1 tbsp | ½ cup |
| Beets | 2½ lbs | Cut in 1-in pieces | 1 tbsp | ½ cup |
| Broccoli | 1 head | Whole, remove stem | 1 tbsp | ½ cup |
| Brussels sprouts | 2 lbs | Cut in half, trim ends | 2 tbsp | ½ cup |
| Carrots | 2½ lbs | Cut in 1-in pieces | 1 tbsp | ½ cup |
| Cauliflower | 1 head | Whole, remove stem | 1 tbsp | ½ cup |
| Parsnip | 2½ lbs | Cut in 1-in pieces | 1 tbsp | ½ cup |
| Potatoes, russet | 2 lbs | Cut in 1-inch wedges | 1 tbsp | ½ cup |
| | 2 lbs | Hand-cut fries, soak 30 mins in cold water then pat dry | 1 tbsp | ½ cup |
| | 4 | Whole (medium) poked several times with a fork | | 1 cup |
| | | Whole (large) poked several times with a fork | | 1 cup |
| | 2½ lbs | Cut in 1-inch pieces | 1 tbsp | ½ cup |
| Spaghetti squash | 1 small squash | Cut in half, remove seeds, puncture with fork about 10 times | 1 tbsp | 2 cups |
| Sweet potatoes | 2½ lbs | Cut in 1-in pieces | 1 tbsp | ½ cup |
| **FRESH BEEF** | | | | |
| Roast beef | 2-3 lbs | None | 2 Tbsp | 1 cup |
| Tenderloin | 2-3 lbs | None | 2 Tbsp | 1 cup |

| | | | |
|---|---|---|---|
| Don't forget to add water or stock to create steam and cook your food. | | | |

NOTE: Steam will take approximately 8-12 minutes to build.

| ACCESSORY | TEMP | COOK TIME | FLIP/SHAKE optional |
|---|---|---|---|
| Cook & Crisp™ Basket | 390°F | 15 mins | 10 mins |
| Cook & Crisp Basket | 400°F | 30-35 mins | 10 mins |
| Cook & Crisp Basket | 425°F | 15-20 mins | |
| Cook & Crisp Basket | 450°F | 20-25 mins | 15 mins |
| Cook & Crisp Basket | 400°F | 22-28 mins | 10 mins |
| Cook & Crisp Basket | 425°F | 23-25 mins | |
| Cook & Crisp Basket | 400°F | 30-35 mins | 20 mins |
| Cook & Crisp Basket | 450°F | 25-30 mins | 20 mins |
| Cook & Crisp Basket | 450°F | 30-35 mins | 25 mins |
| Cook & Crisp Basket | 400°F | 30-35 mins | |
| Cook & Crisp Basket | 400°F | 40-48 mins | |
| Cook & Crisp Basket | 450°F | 30-35 mins | 20 mins |
| Reversible rack, higher position | 375°F | 25-30 mins | |
| Cook & Crisp Basket | 450°F | 30-35 mins | 10 mins |
| Deluxe Reversible Rack, lower position | 365°F | 45 minutes for Medium Rare | |
| Deluxe Reversible Rack, lower position | 365°F | 25-30 minutes for Medium Rare | |

# Steam & Crisp Chart, continued

Steaming & Crisping is a great way to get food that has a crispy exterior but is juicy inside. Before placing the food and accessory into the unit, ensure that you've added water to the bottom of the cooking pot. This is important to ensure that steam will be produced and get you those delicious results you desire.

| INGREDIENT | AMOUNT | PREPARATION | OIL optional | WATER |
|---|---|---|---|---|
| **POULTRY** | | | | |
| Whole chicken | 5–7 lbs | Trussed | Brushed with oil | 1 cup |
| Turkey drumstricks | 2 lbs | None | Brushed with oil | 1 cup |
| Turkey breast | 1 (3–5 lbs) | None | Brushed with oil | 1 cup |
| Chicken breasts (boneless) | 4 breasts, 6–8 oz each | Brush with oil | 2 tbsp | ½ cup |
| Chicken breasts (bone in, skin on) | 4 breasts, ¾–1 ½ lbs each | Brush with oil | 2 tbsp | ½ cup |
| Chicken thighs (bone in) | 4 thighs, 6–10 oz each | Brush with oil | 2 tbsp | ½ cup |
| Chicken thighs (boneless) | 6 thighs, 4–8 oz each | Brush with oil | 2 tbsp | ½ cup |
| Chicken drumsticks | 2 lbs | Brush with oil | 2 tbsp | ½ cup |
| Hand-breaded chicken breasts | 4 breasts, 6 oz each | | | ½ cup |
| Chicken wings | I lb (approx. 21 pieces) | | | ½ cup |
| **PORK** | | | | |
| Fresh pork tenderloins | 2 (1 lb each) | None | 2 Tbsp | 1 cup |
| Pork loin | 1 (2 lbs) | None | 2 Tbsp | 1 cup |
| Spiral ham, bone in | 1 (3 lbs) | None | 2 Tbsp | 1 cup |
| Pork chops, boneless | 4 chops, 6–8 oz each | | 2 tbsp | ½ cup |
| Pork chops (bone in, thick cut) | 2 chops, 10–12 oz each | | 2 tbsp | ½ cup |
| **FISH** | | | | |
| Cod | 4 fillets, 6 oz each | | 1 tbsp | ½ cup |
| Salmon | 4 fillets, 6 oz each | | 1 tbsp | ¼ cup |
| Scallops | 1 lb (approx. 21 pieces) | | 1 tbsp | ¼ cup |

Don't forget to add water or stock to create steam and cook your food.

**NOTE:** Steam will take approximately 8–12 minutes to build.

| ACCESSORY | TEMP | COOK TIME | FLIP/SHAKE optional |
|---|---|---|---|
| Cook and Crisp™ Basket | 365°F | 60–80 mins | |
| Cook and Crisp Basket | 400°F | 32–38 mins | |
| Cook and Crisp Basket | 365°F | 45–55 mins | |
| Deluxe Reversible Rack, higher position | 385°F | 15–20 mins | |
| Deluxe Reversible Rack, higher position | 375°F | 20–25 mins | |
| Deluxe Reversible Rack, higher position | 400°F | 20–25 mins | |
| Deluxe Reversible Rack, higher position | 375°F | 15–18 mins | |
| Cook & Crisp Basket | 425°F | 20–25 mins | 15 mins |
| Deluxe Reversible Rack, higher position | 385°F | 18–20 mins | |
| Cook & Crisp Basket | 450°F | 20–25 mins | |
| Deluxe Reversible Rack, lower position | 375°F | 25–30 mins | |
| Deluxe Reversible Rack, lower position | 365°F | 35–40 mins | |
| Deluxe Reversible Rack, lower position | 325°F | 45–50 mins | |
| Cook & Crisp Basket | 385°F | 20–25 mins | |
| Cook & Crisp Basket | 375°F | 25–30 mins | |
| Deluxe Reversible Rack, higher position | 450°F | 9–12 mins | |
| Deluxe Reversible Rack, higher position | 450°F | 7–10 mins | |
| Deluxe Reversible Rack, higher position | 400°F | 4–6 mins | |

# Steam & Crisp Chart, continued

Steaming & Crisping is a great way to get food that has a crispy exterior but is juicy inside.
Before placing the food and accessory into the unit, ensure that you've added water to the bottom of
the cooking pot. This is important to ensure that steam will be produced and get you those delicious
results you desire.

| INGREDIENT | AMOUNT | PREPARATION | OIL optional | WATER |
| --- | --- | --- | --- | --- |
| **FROZEN BEEF** | | | | |
| Frozen NY Strip Steak | 2 steaks, 10-14 oz each | 2 tbsp canola oil, salt, pepper | | ¾ cup |
| Frozen pork chops, boneless | 4, 6-8 oz each | | 2 tbsp | ½ cup |
| **FROZEN FISH** | | | | |
| Frozen Salmon | 4 fillets, 6 oz each | | 2 tbsp | ½ cup |
| Frozen Shrimp | 18 shrimp, 1 lb | | 2 tbsp | ½ cup |
| Frozen Cod | 4 fillets, 6 oz each | | 2 tbsp | ½ cup |
| Frozen Lobster tails | 4 | | 2 tbsp | ½ cup |
| **FROZEN PORK** | | | | |
| Frozen pork tenderloins | 2 (1 lb each) | None | 2 Tbsp | 1 ½ cups |
| Pork loin | 1 (2 lbs) | None | 2 Tbsp | None |
| Frozen pork chops, boneless | 4, 6-8 oz each | | 2 tbsp | ½ cup |
| Frozen Pork Chops, bone-in, thick cut | 2, 10-12 oz each | | 2 tbsp | ¾ cup |
| Frozen Italian sausages | 6 uncooked | | 2 tbsp | ½ cup |
| **FROZEN PREPARED FOODS** | | | | |
| Dumplings/Pot stickers | 16 oz bag | | 2 tbsp | ½ cup |
| Ravioli | 25 oz bag | | 2 tbsp | ½ cup |
| Eggrolls | 10 oz pkg | | | ½ cup |

> Don't forget to add water or stock to create steam and cook your food.

**NOTE:** Steam will take approximately 8-12 minutes to build.

| ACCESSORY | TEMP | COOK TIME | FLIP/SHAKE *optional* |
|---|---|---|---|
| Deluxe Reversible Rack, lower position | 400°F | 22-28 mins | 20 mins |
| Deluxe Reversible Rack, higher position | 375°F | 15-20 mins | |
| Deluxe Reversible Rack, higher position | 450°F | 11-15 mins | |
| Cook & Crisp Basket | 450°F | 2-5 mins | |
| Deluxe Reversible Rack, higher position | 450°F | 10-15 mins | |
| Deluxe Reversible Rack, higher position | 450°F | 5-7 mins | |
| Deluxe Reversible Rack, lower position | 365°F | 30-35 mins | |
| Deluxe Reversible Rack, lower position | 360°F | 37-40 mins | |
| Deluxe Reversible Rack, higher position | 375°F | 15-20 mins | |
| Deluxe Reversible Rack, higher position | 365°F | 23-28 mins | |
| Deluxe Reversible Rack, higher position | 375°F | 10-12 mins | |
| Cook & Crisp Basket | 400°F | 12-16 mins | 8 mins |
| Cook & Crisp Basket | 385°F | 12-16 mins | |
| Cook & Crisp Basket | 400°F | 15-20 mins | |

# TenderCrisp® Chart

| PROTEIN | AMOUNT | ACCESSORY |
|---|---|---|
| Whole chicken | 1 chicken (6-7 lbs) | Cook & Crisp™ Basket |
| St. Louis ribs | 1 rack, cut in quarters | Cook & Crisp Basket |
| Frozen chicken breasts | 2 breasts (6-8 oz each) | Deluxe Reversible Rack, higher position |
| Frozen New York strip steaks | 2 steaks (12 oz each) | Deluxe Reversible Rack, higher position |
| | 2 steaks (14 oz each) | Deluxe Reversible Rack, higher position |
| | 2 steaks (16 oz each) | Deluxe Reversible Rack, higher position |
| Frozen chicken wings | 1 lb | Cook & Crisp Basket |
| Frozen pork chops | 4 chops (6-8 oz each) | Deluxe Reversible Rack, higher position |
| Frozen jumbo shrimp | 28 uncooked, peeled, deveined | Deluxe Reversible Rack, Deluxe Layer installed, place shrimp on both layers |

 **Don't forget to add water or stock to create steam and cook your food.**

| WATER | PRESSURE COOK | PRESSURE RELEASE | |
|-------|---------------|------------------|---|
| 1 cup | High for 40 mins | | Air Fry at 400°F for 15 mins |
| 1 cup | High for 19 mins, quick release | | Air Fry at 400°F for 10-15 mins |
| 1 cup | High for 10 mins, quick release | After quick release, move slider to AIR FRY/STOVETOP position and open lid. | Broil for 10 mins |
| 1 cup | High for 1 min, quick release | | Broil for 8-10 mins |
| 1 cup | High for 2 mins, quick release | Pat protein dry with paper towel, brush with oil or sauce and season as desired. | Broil for 8-10 mins |
| 1 cup | High for 3 mins, quick release | | Broil for 8-10 mins |
| 1 cup | High for 5 mins, quick release | Close lid and continue to cook as instructed. | Air Fry at 390°F for 15-20 mins |
| 1 cup | High for 2 mins, quick release | | Air Fry at 400°F for 8-12 mins |
| 1 cup | High for 0 mins, quick release | | Air Fry at 400°F for 5 mins |

# Pressure Cook Chart

TIP Use hot water for pressure cooking to build pressure quicker.

| INGREDIENT | WEIGHT | PREPARATION |
| --- | --- | --- |
| **POULTRY** | | |
| Chicken breasts | 2 lbs | Bone in |
| | 6 small or 4 large (about 2 lbs) | Boneless |
| Chicken breasts (frozen) | 4 large (2 lbs) | Boneless |
| Chicken thighs | 8 thighs (4 lbs) | Bone in/skin on |
| | 8 thighs (2 lbs) | Boneless |
| Chicken, whole | 4–5 lbs | Bone in/legs tied |
| Turkey breast | 1 breast (6–8 lbs) | Bone in |
| **GROUND MEAT** | | |
| Ground beef, pork, or turkey | 1–2 lbs | Ground (not in patties) |
| Ground beef, pork, or turkey (frozen) | 1–2 lbs | Frozen, ground (not in patties) |
| **RIBS** | | |
| Pork baby back | 2 1/2–3 1/2 lbs | Cut in thirds |
| **ROASTS** | | |
| Beef brisket | 3–4 lbs | Whole |
| Boneless beef chuck-eye roast | 3–4 lbs | Whole |
| Boneless pork butt | 4 lbs | Season as desired |
| Pork tenderloin | 2 tenderloins (1–1 1/2 lbs each) | Season as desired |
| **STEW MEAT** | | |
| Boneless beef short ribs | 6 ribs (3 lbs) | Whole |
| Boneless leg of lamb | 3 lbs | Cut in 1-inch pieces |
| Boneless pork butt | 3 lbs | Cut in 1-inch pieces |
| Chuck roast, for stew | 2 lbs | Cut in 1-inch pieces |
| **EGGS** | | |
| Hard-boiled eggs† | 1–12 eggs | None |

†Remove immediately when complete and place in ice bath.

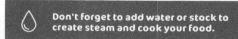
Don't forget to add water or stock to create steam and cook your food.

| WATER | ACCESSORY | PRESSURE | TIME | RELEASE |
|---|---|---|---|---|
| | | | | |
| 1 cup | N/A | High | 15 mins | Quick |
| 1 cup | N/A | High | 8-10 mins | Quick |
| 1 cup | N/A | High | 25 mins | Quick |
| 1 cup | N/A | High | 20 mins | Quick |
| 1 cup | N/A | High | 20 mins | Quick |
| 1 cup | Cook & Crisp™ Basket | High | 25-30 mins | Quick |
| 1 cup | N/A | High | 40-50 mins | Quick |
| | | | | |
| 1 cup | N/A | High | 5 mins | Quick |
| 1 cup | N/A | High | 20-25 mins | Quick |
| | | | | |
| 1 cup | N/A | High | 20 mins | Quick |
| | | | | |
| 1 cup | N/A | High | 1-1 1/2 hrs | Quick |
| 1 cup | N/A | High | 1-1 1/2 hrs | Quick |
| 1 cup | N/A | High | 1 1/2 hrs | Quick |
| 1 cup | N/A | High | 3-4 mins | Quick |
| | | | | |
| 1 cup | N/A | High | 25 mins | Quick |
| 1 cup | N/A | High | 30 mins | Quick |
| 1 cup | N/A | High | 30 mins | Quick |
| 1 cup | N/A | High | 25 mins | Quick |
| | | | | |
| 1 cup | N/A | High | 4 mins | Quick |

# Pressure Cook Chart, continued

| INGREDIENT | AMOUNT | PREPARATION |
|---|---|---|
| **VEGETABLES** | | |
| Beets | 8 small or 4 large | Rinse well, trim tops and ends; cool and peel after cooking |
| Broccoli | 1 head or 4 cups | Cut in 1–2-inch florets, remove stem |
| Brussels sprouts | 1 lb | Cut in half |
| Butternut squash (cubed for side dish or salad) | 32 oz (2 lbs) | Peel, cut in 1-inch pieces, remove seeds |
| Butternut squash (for mashed, puree, or soup) | 32 oz | Peel, cut in 1-inch pieces, remove seeds |
| Cabbage (braised) | 1 head | Cut in half, slice in ½-inch strips, remove core |
| Cabbage (crisp) | 1 head | Cut in half, slice in ½-inch strips, remove core |
| Carrots | 1 lb | Peel, cut in ½-inch pieces |
| Cauliflower | 1 head | Cut in 1–2-inch florets, remove stem |
| Collard greens | 2 bunches or 1 bag (16 oz) | Remove stems, chop leaves |
| Green beans | 1 bag (12 oz) | Whole |
| Kale leaves/greens | 2 bunches or 1 bag (16 oz) | Remove stems, chop leaves |
| Potatoes, red (cubed for side dish or salad) | 2 lbs | Scrub, cut in 1-inch cubes |
| Potatoes, red (for mashed) | 2 lbs | Scrub, whole, large potatoes cut in half |
| Potatoes, russet or Yukon (cubed for side dish or salad) | 2 lbs | Peel, cut in 1-inch cubes |
| Potatoes, russet or Yukon (for mashed) | 2 lbs | Peel, cut in 1-inch thick slices |
| Potatoes, sweet (cubed for side dish or salad) | 2 lbs | Peel, cut in 1-inch cubes |
| Potatoes, sweet (for mashed) | 2 lbs | Peel, cut in 1-inch thick slices |
| **DOUBLE-CAPACITY VEGETABLES** | | |
| Broccoli | 2 heads or 8 cups | Cut in 1–2-inch florets, remove stem |
| Brussels sprouts | 2 lbs | Cut in half, remove stem |
| Butternut squash | 48 oz | Peel, cut in 1-inch pieces |
| Cabbage | 1 ½ heads | Cut in half, remove core |
| Green beans | 2 bags (24 oz) | Whole |

*The time the unit takes to pressurize is long enough to cook this food.

| WATER | ACCESSORY | PRESSURE | COOK TIME | RELEASE |
|-------|-----------|----------|-----------|---------|
| 1 cup | N/A | High | 15–20 mins | Quick |
| 1 cup | Deluxe Reversible Rack, lower position | Low | 1 min | Quick |
| 1 cup | Deluxe Reversible Rack, lower position | Low | 1 min | Quick |
| 1 cup | Cook & Crisp™ Basket | Low | 2 mins | Quick |
| 1 cup | N/A | High | 2 mins | Quick |
| 1 cup | N/A | Low | 3 mins | Quick |
| 1 cup | Cook & Crisp Basket | Low | 2 mins | Quick |
| 1 cup | N/A | High | 2–3 mins | Quick |
| 1 cup | Cook & Crisp Basket | Low | 1 min | Quick |
| 1 cup | N/A | Low | 6 mins | Quick |
| 1 cup | Cook & Crisp Basket | Low | 0 mins* | Quick |
| 1 cup | N/A | Low | 3 mins | Quick |
| 1 cup | Cook & Crisp Basket | High | 1–2 mins | Quick |
| 1 cup | N/A | High | 15–20 mins | Quick |
| 1 cup | Cook & Crisp Basket | High | 1–2 mins | Quick |
| 1 cup | N/A | High | 6 mins | Quick |
| 1 cup | Cook & Crisp Basket | High | 1–2 mins | Quick |
| 1 cup | N/A | High | 6 mins | Quick |
| 1 cup | Deluxe Reversible Rack (both layers) | Low | 1 min | Quick |
| 1 cup | Deluxe Reversible Rack (both layers) | Low | 1 min | Quick |
| 1 cup | Deluxe Reversible Rack (both layers) | High | 3 mins | Quick |
| 1 cup | Deluxe Reversible Rack (both layers) | Low | 5 mins | Quick |
| 1 cup | Deluxe Reversible Rack (both layers) | Low | 0 mins* | Quick |

# Pressure Cook Chart, continued

| INGREDIENTS | AMOUNT | WATER |
|---|---|---|
| **GRAINS** | | |
| Arborio rice* | 1 cup | 3 cups |
| Basmati rice | 1 cup | 1 cup |
| Brown rice, short/medium or long grain | 1 cup | 1 1/4 cups |
| Coarse grits/polenta* | 1 cup | 5 1/2 cups |
| Farro | 1 cup | 2 cups |
| Jasmine rice | 1 cup | 1 cup |
| Kamut | 1 cup | 2 cups |
| Millet | 1 cup | 2 cups |
| Pearl barley | 1 cup | 2 cups |
| Quinoa | 1 cup | 1 1/2 cups |
| Quinoa, red | 1 cup | 1 1/2 cups |
| Spelt | 1 cup | 2 1/2 cups |
| Steel-cut oats* | 1 cup | 3 cups |
| Sushi rice | 1 cup | 1 1/2 cups |
| Texmati® rice, brown** | 1 cup | 1 1/4 cups |
| Texmati® rice, light brown** | 1 cup | 1 1/4 cups |
| Texmati® rice, white** | 1 cup | 1 cup |
| Wheat berries | 1 cup | 3 cups |
| White rice, long grain | 1 cup | 1 cup |
| White rice, medium grain | 1 cup | 1 cup |
| Wild rice | 1 cup | 2 cups |

*After releasing pressure, stir for 30 seconds to 1 minute, then let sit for 5 minutes.

**TEXMATI is a registered trademark of Riviana Foods, Inc. Use of the TEXMATI trademark does not imply any affiliation with or endorsement by Riviana Foods, Inc.

**Don't forget to add water or stock to create steam and cook your food.**

| PRESSURE | COOK TIME | RELEASE |
|----------|-----------|---------|
| High | 4 mins | Delayed (10 mins) |
| High | 2 mins | Delayed (10 mins) |
| High | 15 mins | Delayed (10 mins) |
| High | 4 mins | Delayed (10 mins) |
| High | 10 mins | Delayed (10 mins) |
| High | 2–3 mins | Delayed (10 mins) |
| High | 30 mins | Delayed (10 mins) |
| High | 6 mins | Delayed (10 mins) |
| High | 22 mins | Delayed (10 mins) |
| High | 2 mins | Delayed (10 mins) |
| High | 2 mins | Delayed (10 mins) |
| High | 25 mins | Delayed (10 mins) |
| High | 11 mins | Delayed (10 mins) |
| High | 3 mins | Delayed (10 mins) |
| High | 5 mins | Delayed (10 mins) |
| High | 2 mins | Delayed (10 mins) |
| High | 2 mins | Delayed (10 mins) |
| High | 15 mins | Delayed (10 mins) |
| High | 2 mins | Delayed (10 mins) |
| High | 3 mins | Delayed (10 mins) |
| High | 22 mins | Delayed (10 mins) |

# Pressure Cook Chart, continued

| INGREDIENTS | AMOUNT | WATER |
|---|---|---|
| **LEGUMES** | | |
| All beans, except lentils, should be soaked 8–24 hours before cooking. | | |
| Black beans | 1 lb, soaked 8–24 hrs | 6 cups |
| Black-eyed peas | 1 lb, soaked 8–24 hrs | 6 cups |
| Cannellini beans | 1 lb, soaked 8–24 hrs | 6 cups |
| Cranberry beans | 1 lb, soaked 8–24 hrs | 6 cups |
| Garbanzo beans (chickpeas) | 1 lb, soaked 8–24 hrs | 6 cups |
| Great northern bean | 1 lb, soaked 8–24 hrs | 6 cups |
| Lentils (green or brown) | 1 cup dry | 2 cups |
| Lima beans | 1 lb, soaked 8–24 hrs | 6 cups |
| Navy beans | 1 lb, soaked 8–24 hrs | 6 cups |
| Pinto beans | 1 lb, soaked 8–24 hrs | 6 cups |
| Red kidney beans | 1 lb, soaked 8–24 hrs | 6 cups |
| This section does not require beans to be soaked. | | |
| Black beans | 2 lbs | 4 quarts (16 cups) |
| Black-eyed peas | 2 lbs | 4 quarts (16 cups) |
| Cannellini beans | 2 lbs | 4 quarts (16 cups) |
| Cranberry beans | 2 lbs | 4 quarts (16 cups) |
| Garbanzo beans (chickpeas) | 2 lbs | 4 quarts (16 cups) |
| Great northern bean | 2 lbs | 4 quarts (16 cups) |
| Lima beans | 2 lbs | 4 quarts (16 cups) |
| Navy beans | 2 lbs | 4 quarts (16 cups) |
| Pinto beans | 2 lbs | 4 quarts (16 cups) |
| Red kidney beans | 2 lbs | 4 quarts (16 cups) |

 **Don't forget to add water or stock to create steam and cook your food.**

> TIP Cover beans with 3 inches of water, soak overnight, then drain and rinse thoroughly. Return the beans to pot and cover with the amount of water designated in the chart below.

| PRESSURE | COOK TIME | RELEASE |
| --- | --- | --- |
| Low | 5 mins | Delayed (10 mins) |
| Low | 5 mins | Delayed (10 mins) |
| Low | 3 mins | Delayed (10 mins) |
| Low | 3 mins | Delayed (10 mins) |
| Low | 3 mins | Delayed (10 mins) |
| Low | 1 min | Delayed (10 mins) |
| Low | 5 mins | Delayed (10 mins) |
| Low | 1 min | Delayed (10 mins) |
| Low | 3 mins | Delayed (10 mins) |
| Low | 3 mins | Delayed (10 mins) |
| Low | 3 mins | Delayed (10 mins) |
| High | 25 mins | Delayed (15 mins) |
| High | 25 mins | Delayed (15 mins) |
| High | 40 mins | Delayed (15 mins) |
| High | 40 mins | Delayed (15 mins) |
| High | 40 mins | Delayed (15 mins) |
| High | 30 mins | Delayed (15 mins) |
| High | 30 mins | Delayed (15 mins) |
| High | 30 mins | Delayed (15 mins) |
| High | 30 mins | Delayed (15 mins) |
| High | 40 mins | Delayed (15 mins) |

# Air Fry Chart for the Cook & Crisp™ Basket

| INGREDIENT | AMOUNT | PREPARATION |
|---|---|---|
| **VEGETABLES** | | |
| Asparagus | 1 bunch | Cut in half, trim stems |
| Beets | 6 small or 4 large (about 2 lbs) | Whole |
| Bell peppers (for roasting) | 4 peppers | Whole |
| Broccoli | 1 head | Cut in 1-2-inch florets |
| Brussels sprouts | 1 lb | Cut in half, remove stems |
| Butternut squash | 1-1 1/2 lbs | Cut in 1-2-inch pieces |
| Carrots | 1 lb | Peeled, cut in 1/2-inch pieces |
| Cauliflower | 1 head | Cut in 1-2-inch florets |
| Corn on the cob | 4 ears, cut in half | Whole, remove husks |
| Green beans | 1 bag (12 oz) | Trimmed |
| Kale (for chips) | 6 cups, packed | Tear in pieces, remove stems |
| Mushrooms | 8 oz | Rinse, cut in quarters |
| Potatoes, russet | 1 1/2 lbs | Cut in 1-inch wedges |
| | 1 lb | Hand-cut fries, thin |
| | 1 lb | Hand-cut fries, soak 30 mins in cold water then pat dry |
| | 4 whole (6-8 oz) | Pierce with fork 3 times |
| Potatoes, sweet | 2 lbs | Cut in 1-inch chunks |
| | 4 whole (6-8 oz) | Pierce with fork 3 times |
| Zucchini | 1 lb | Cut in quarters lengthwise, then cut in 1-inch pieces |
| **POULTRY** | | |
| Chicken breasts | 2 breasts (3/4-1 1/2 lbs each) | Bone in |
| | 2 breasts (1/2-3/4 lb each) | Boneless |
| Chicken thighs | 4 thighs (6-10 oz each) | Bone in |
| | 4 thighs (4-8 oz each) | Boneless |
| Chicken wings | 2 lbs | Drumettes & flats |
| Chicken, whole | 1 chicken (4-6 lbs) | Trussed |
| Chicken drumsticks | 2 lbs | None |

| | | |
|---|---|---|
| TIP Before using Air Fry, allow the unit to preheat for 5 minutes as you would your conventional oven. | | |

| OIL | TEMP | COOK TIME |
|---|---|---|
| 2 tsp | 390°F | 8–10 mins |
| None | 390°F | 45–60 mins |
| None | 400°F | 25–30 mins |
| 1 Tbsp | 390°F | 10–13 mins |
| 1 Tbsp | 390°F | 15–18 mins |
| 1 Tbsp | 390°F | 20–25 mins |
| 1 Tbsp | 390°F | 14–16 mins |
| 2 Tbsp | 390°F | 15–20 mins |
| 1 Tbsp | 390°F | 12–15 mins |
| 1 Tbsp | 390°F | 7–10 mins |
| None | 300°F | 8–11 mins |
| 1 Tbsp | 390°F | 7–8 mins |
| 1 Tbsp | 390°F | 20–25 mins |
| ½–3 Tbsp canola | 390°F | 20–25 mins |
| ½–3 Tbsp canola | 390°F | 24–27 mins |
| None | 390°F | 35–40 mins |
| 1 Tbsp | 390°F | 15–20 mins |
| None | 390°F | 35–40 mins |
| 1 Tbsp | 390°F | 15–20 mins |
| Brushed with oil | 375°F | 25–35 mins |
| Brushed with oil | 375°F | 22–25 mins |
| Brushed with oil | 390°F | 22–28 mins |
| Brushed with oil | 390°F | 18–22 mins |
| 1 Tbsp | 390°F | 24–28 mins |
| Brushed with oil | 375°F | 55–75 mins |
| 1 Tbsp | 390°F | 20–22 mins |

# Air Fry Chart for the Cook & Crisp™ Basket, continued

| INGREDIENT | AMOUNT | PREPARATION |
|---|---|---|
| **BEEF** | | |
| Burgers | 4 quarter-pound patties, 80% lean | 1-inch thick |
| Steaks | 2 steaks (8 oz each) | Whole |
| **PORK & LAMB** | | |
| Bacon | 1 strip to 1 (16 oz) package | Lay strips evenly over edge of basket |
| Pork chops | 2 thick-cut, bone-in chops (10-12 oz each) | Bone in |
| | 4 boneless chops (6-8 oz each) | Boneless |
| Pork tenderloins | 2 tenderloins (1-1 1/2 lbs each) | Whole |
| Sausages | 4 sausages | Whole |
| **FISH & SEAFOOD** | | |
| Crab cakes | 2 cakes (6-8 oz each) | None |
| Lobster tails | 4 tails (3-4 oz each) | Whole |
| Salmon fillets | 2 fillets (4 oz each) | None |
| Shrimp | 16 jumbo | Raw, whole, peel, keep tails on |
| **FROZEN FOODS** | | |
| Chicken nuggets | 1 box (12 oz) | None |
| Fish fillets | 1 box (6 fillets) | None |
| Fish sticks | 1 box (14.8 oz) | None |
| French fries | 1 lb | None |
| | 2 lbs | None |
| Mozzarella sticks | 1 box (11 oz) | None |
| Pot stickers | 1 bag (10 count) | None |
| Pizza Rolls | 1 bag (20 oz, 40 count) | None |
| Popcorn shrimp | 1 box (16 oz) | None |
| Tater Tots | 1 lb | None |

TIP Before using Air Fry, allow the unit to preheat for 5 minutes as you would your conventional oven.

| OIL | TEMP | COOK TIME |
|---|---|---|
| None | 375°F | 10-12 mins |
| None | 390°F | 10-20 mins |
| None | 330°F | 13-16 mins (no preheat) |
| Brushed with oil | 375°F | 15-17 mins |
| Brushed with oil | 375°F | 15-18 mins |
| Brushed with oil | 375°F | 25-35 mins |
| None | 390°F | 8-10 mins |
| Brushed with oil | 350°F | 10-13 mins |
| None | 375°F | 7-10 mins |
| Brushed with oil | 390°F | 10-13 mins |
| 1 Tbsp | 390°F | 7-10 mins |
| None | 390°F | 11-13 mins |
| None | 390°F | 13-15 mins |
| None | 390°F | 9-11 mins |
| None | 360°F | 18-22 mins |
| None | 360°F | 28-32 mins |
| None | 375°F | 6-9 mins |
| Toss with 1 tsp canola oil | 390°F | 11-14 mins |
| None | 390°F | 12-15 mins |
| None | 390°F | 8-10 mins |
| None | 360°F | 19-22 mins |

# INDEX

# ABOUT THE AUTHORS

## *THE NINJA TEST KITCHEN*

The Ninja Test Kitchen is composed of a team of diverse chefs, each with a unique background. They spend hours upon hours testing Ninja's appliance prototypes. Every decision regarding our products and our recipes is made with you in mind—how it will improve your life and your experience in the kitchen. The Ninja Test Kitchen's goal is to make all the mistakes so that you don't have to. We find joy in transforming the way you cook and developing recipes that will allow you to fall in love with our projects.

Meet the Ninja Test Kitchen team.

## KENZIE SWANHART

*Director, Global Culinary Innovation, and Head of the Ninja Test Kitchen*

**Kenzie Swanhart** is a home cook turned food blogger and cookbook author, providing her readers with inspiration both in and out of the kitchen. With more than 350,000 copies of her cookbooks in print, Kenzie never wavers in her mission: creating easy, flavorful recipes made with wholesome ingredients and sharing them with her readers.

As the head of culinary innovation for Ninja, Kenzie works with her team to provide a unique, food-first point of view for the development of new products and recipes to make consumers' lives easier and healthier. You'll also see her serving as the face of Ninja on the leading television home shopping network, where she shares tips, tricks, and recipes for the company's full line of products.

Kenzie lives in the Boston area with her husband, Julien, and their dogs, Charlie and Milo.

## SAM FERGUSON

*Manager, Culinary Product Innovation*

**Sam Ferguson** is a culinary innovation and marketing manager at Ninja, overseeing and leading the culinary product development of heated cooking appliances.

After 10 fulfilling years in the restaurant industry, Sam was ready to step out of the grind of kitchen life and into something less stressful but equally rewarding. Enter Ninja! As a leader on the product development team, Sam strives to create high-quality, innovative, and truly useful cooking tools for home chefs around the world.

Sam lives in Boston with his wife, Lily, and his beagle, Waylon.

## MEG JORDAN

*Manager, Recipe and Culinary Content Development*

**Meg Jordan** is an advertising agency professional turned culinary specialist after making a career change in 2017. After spending most of a decade working in media with *Fortune* 500 clients, Meg decided to pursue her lifelong passion to work in the culinary industry. A graduate of the Boston University Culinary Arts Certificate program, Meg studied under high-profile chefs in the Boston culinary scene as well as with chef Jacques Pépin. Meg joined the Ninja Test Kitchen team in 2018, and in her spare time, she enjoys learning about the art of charcuterie and whole-animal butchery.

## KARA BLEDAY

*Culinary Manager, International*

**Kara Bleday's** love of cooking took her from the lobbying halls of DC to the Culinary Institute of the Pacific in 2010. After culinary school, she interned with chef Masaharu Morimoto at his Waikiki restaurant, immersing herself in Asian cuisine and cooking techniques. Soon after, while living in Guam, Kara traveled throughout Asia and the Pacific learning about new and old food trends, studying different markets, and understanding how the culinary world is interwoven. Kara launched Ninja's first ever Global Chef Network and London's Test Kitchen, bringing 5-star products to consumers around the globe.

Kara then relocated to upstate New York. There, while working for a local restaurant group, she opened a restaurant as a private consultant. Then, after building a consulting business in San Diego, Kara and her husband relocated to Boston, where they live with their two sons.

## CRAIG WHITE

*Culinary Manager, Motorized*

**Craig White's** love for cooking can be traced back to when he was four years old and his mother caught him cooking hot dogs in the middle of the night. A Le Cordon Bleu graduate, he was given his first chance in a kitchen by chef Jody Adams at Rialto in Boston. He has worked under James Beard Award–winning chefs Nancy Silverton of Mozza in Los Angeles and Frank McClelland of FRANK in Beverly, Massachusetts. He opened and owned Half Baked Cafe and Bakery in Beverly Farms. After two years as chef de cuisine at Ledger in Salem, he joined Ninja as a consultant and is now research chef for Ninja Motorized. Through his cooking he has been "positively impacting people's lives every day," and he is excited to do it "in every home around the world" with Ninja.

Craig lives in Salem, Massachusetts, with his girlfriend, Michelle. In his free time, he enjoys traveling, collecting cookbooks, fishing, and playing guitar.

## MELISSA CELLI

*Senior Research Chef*

**Melissa Celli** is a New Jersey native who came to Ninja after a 15-year career in the food industry. Her love of food and cooking began in childhood while observing her mother cook many meals and desserts for her family. After graduating with a bachelor's degree in food service management and culinary arts from Johnson & Wales University in 2009, Melissa went on to work for the likes of Wegmans Food Markets, Walt Disney World, Steritech, Compass Group, and Whole Foods Market in various cooking, food safety, and management roles. Melissa's love for being a part of a food research and development team is what drew her to Ninja, as well as the escape from the everyday grind of the restaurant lifestyle. She is one of the lead culinary developers on Ninja® Heated.

Melissa lives in Framingham, Massachusetts, with her husband, Alfredo, and their dog, Carmella.

## KELLY GRAY

*Research Chef*

**Kelly Gray** is a food scientist and travel enthusiast whose cooking style is influenced by childhood nostalgia and other cultures. Her experience spans many aspects of the food industry, from restaurant work to baking mix formulation—even shellfish farming! As an alumna of California State Polytechnic University, Pomona, with a degree in food science and technology and culinology, Kelly has a culinary approach that is as analytical as it is creative—quite useful in her current role in the Ninja Test Kitchen. As a believer in the relationship between good food, community, and well-being, Kelly hopes to encourage people to come back to the kitchen with approachable recipes and state-of-the-art appliances that make cooking enjoyable and stress-free.

When she's not in the test kitchen or cooking for her friends and family, you can find Kelly enjoying the outdoors, salsa dancing, or daydreaming about a trip to someplace new.

## CAROLINE SCHLIEP

*Research Chef*

**Caroline Schliep** is a Midwest native turned New Englander who has had a passion for cooking since a young age. Her love of travel has led her to work at many restaurants around the country, even studying abroad in Singapore and Thailand with At-Sunrice GlobalChef Academy. She is an alumna of Johnson & Wales University in Providence, Rhode Island, where she earned an associate's degree in culinary arts and a bachelor's degree in culinary nutrition and food science. Nowadays you can find her in the Ninja Test Kitchen, where she takes on many roles, from product development and testing to recipe development and validation.

## ATHIA LANDRY

*Recipe and Content Developer*

**Athia Landry's** interest in plant-based cooking started over a decade ago and quickly became her career. With a degree in art history, she enjoys combining her passions for art and food through recipe development, writing, and food styling.

Her experience in plant-based home cooking has given her the opportunity to develop and style recipes for the vegan meal kit company Purple Carrot. With an appreciation for the finer details, she enjoys curating dinner menus for friends and family and mastering the art of making macarons. Athia joined the Ninja Test Kitchen team in 2020 and is excited to help bring the Ninja story to life through recipe and content development.

## MYLES BRYAN

*Kitchen Assistant*

**Myles Bryan** is originally from New York, which is where his passion for food started. He is a Johnson & Wales University graduate with an associate's degree in culinary science and a bachelor's degree in food service management. Myles has experience working in various boutique restaurants and country clubs. He has even had the privilege of organizing a dinner for the James Beard House in New York City.

He also achieved bronze in a Federazione Italiana Cuochi cooking competition hosted in Rimini, Italy. In his free time, he enjoys photography and cooking for his friends and family. He is delighted to be on the Ninja Test Kitchen team and looks forward to developing more recipes.

## JENNIE VINCENT

*Research and Development Chef, International*

Having inherited a love of both food and travel from her father, **Jennie Vincent** chose to train as a chef at Westminster College, London, before going on to study at the Wine and Spirits Education Trust. This led her to a career in hospitality, including working in both Australia and the United States. Jennie then made the choice to open her own café in London, but after 10 years she decided on a career change. This led her to working freelance as a food stylist, recipe developer, and consultant for companies such as Waitrose and the BBC, as well as leading food publications, cookbooks, and advertisements. In 2020, Jennie joined Ninja as a research and development chef in London. In her spare time, she can be found experimenting in the kitchen, traveling, or cycling around London looking for something delicious to eat.

## AVERY LOWE

*Research Chef*

**Avery Lowe's** curiosity and passion for all things culinary was a clearly determined path, stretching back to her early days on the school bus where she would interview her friends and seatmates on what they had for dinner the night prior. This hunger and desire to instill a love for food in everyone around her set Avery on a professional quest to cook, learn, and always be around food. Her culinary journey started at America's Test Kitchen, where she worked on the Kitchen Operations team as the senior kitchen assistant, absorbing knowledge of specialty-ingredient procurement and the recipe development process. In 2021, Avery joined the Ninja Test Kitchen, where she works as a research chef on the Motorized team. She happily spends her days drinking smoothies and working to make the home cook's experience in the kitchen more fulfilling. In her spare time, you can find her writing (Avery received her bachelor's degree in English from Connecticut College in 2018), riding her bike, playing guitar, and, of course, cooking for her family and friends.

## MICHELLE BOLAND

*Research Chef*

After 12 years in the restaurant industry, executive pastry chef turned research chef **Michelle Boland** joined the Ninja Test Kitchen in early 2021. From bakeries to fine dining restaurants, Michelle spent most of her career crafting her personal style in the form of cakes, pastries, and plated desserts. After winning Star Chefs Rising Star pastry chef, Boston's Best, and NorthShore BONs awards, Michelle decided to make a career change to use more of her critical mind in the development of appliances and recipe writing while also having more time to enjoy life with her friends and family! When not working, Michelle enjoys spending time with her fiancé, Craig, kayaking, and shopping at Marshalls.

Printed in the USA
CPSIA information can be obtained
at www.ICGtesting.com
CBHW051813240424
7401CB00007B/7